MANAGEMENT AND ECONOMIC DEVELOPMENT

STUDIES IN SOCIAL LIFE XVII

EDITOR:
GUNTHER BEYER

MANAGEMENT AND ECONOMIC DEVELOPMENT

THE CASE OF TAIWAN

by

ANANT R. NEGANDHI, PH. D.

MARTINUS NIJHOFF / THE HAGUE / 1973

To our son, Amin

ISBN-13: 978-90-247-5142-6 e-ISBN-13 : 978-94-010-2482-2
DOI: 10.1007/978-94-010-2482-2

TABLE OF CONTENTS

LIST OF TABLES

PREFACE

The ping-pong diplomacy and its aftermath discussion, coupled with the entry of communist China into the United Nations and the subsequent expulsion of Taiwan, will generate considerable political dialogue about the changing balance of power and the fate of the other China. These political discussions will obviously overshadow the true role and function of the existence of Taiwan.

Given the time, Taiwan could become a model for the development process for other emerging countries. Taiwan's experience with economic development has real relevance for many countries. For example, in less than two decades Taiwan has achieved the industrial and economic growth that should well make it the envy of nearly all other developing nations. Its per capita income is exceeded only by Japan among the countries of the Far East. Yet, despite vigorous economic and industrial growth, obvious breakdowns in this economic progress come into view. The lack of managerial input threatens to become a real bottleneck.

The study reported in this volume examines the feasibility and utility of transferring advanced management know-how and practices into the industrial enterprises in Taiwan in order to generate further economic and industrial growth. The study itself concerns management practices and effectiveness of American subsidiaries, Japanese subsidiaries, and comparable local firms in Taiwan.

This was a cooperative study undertaken by Kent State University and Soochow University of Taiwan. It was conducted under the auspices of the Comparative Administration Research Institute and the Center for Business and Economic Research, both in the College of Business Administration at Kent State. The research was supported by the Council for International Economic Cooperation and Development (CIECD), Taipei, Taiwan, the Research Council of Kent State University, and the Center for Business and Economic Research, a research unit in the College of Business Administration at Kent State University. I owe a special acknowledgement of appreciation to these institutions for their financial support.

Only the active encouragement and help of many different individuals and institutions make it possible to undertake and complete research of this nature and it is quite impossible to thank them all. However, I would like to acknowledge my colleagues at Kent State University, Dr. John T. Doutt, Professor of Management, Dr. Bernard Hall, Vice-President and Provost, Dr. Gail Mullin, Dean of the College of Business Administration, and Dr. Robert J. Saunders, then Director of the Center for Business and Economic Research. They were most generous in providing both encouragement and resources for this project.

I would also like to express my deep gratitude to Professor Edward L. Rada, School of Public Health, University of California at Los Angeles, who initiated my interest in undertaking this study. In addition, my colleagues at Soochow University, Dr. Wu Kan and Professor Lamp Li, and Dr. Billy Yang, Dean of the Graduate School of Business and Public Administration at the National Chengchi University, Taipei, Taiwan, provided invaluable assistance and cooperation during the field research in Taiwan. I owe them my sincere appreciation. The Soochow University Campus was our home during this field study and both my wife and I extend our thanks to the administrators and faculty and their families for treating us as one of them. My research assistant in Taiwan, Mr. Robert Hsieh, was not only an extraordinary host but a meticulous researcher and I offer him my special thanks. Sincere appreciation also goes to Barbara Fisher, publications Writer at the Center for Business and Economic Research at Kent State, who smilingly did the dirty work of editing. Last, but certainly not least, I would like to extend my warm regards and gratitude to the executives of those firms participating in this research. They were not only gracious but exceedingly generous with their time and cooperation.

There are no words to thank my wife, Erny, for her never-failing encouragement and patience. Her determination to undertake and complete this research was equal to my own even though she was involved in quite a different project during this time period. The result of that project was a fine son who was born shortly after our return to the United States.

It is to our son, Amin, this book is dedicated. In his own way this tiny boy provided a giant portion of the encouragement necessary to complete my research and ultimately finish this manuscript.

December, 1972 A.R.N.

CHAPTER I

ENTERPRISE MANAGEMENT AND ECONOMIC DEVELOPMENT

About the Book

This book reports the findings of an empirical study undertaken in Taiwan concerning management practices and effectiveness of American subsidiaries, Japanese subsidiaries, and comparable local firms in that country. The main purpose of this study was to examine the feasibility and utility of transferring advanced management practices to developing countries.

The rationale in undertaking this research was based on the premise that, in the march toward industrialization and economic development, the managerial aspect plays an important role in underdeveloped countries; however, thus far it has received very little attention from development theorists. The study reported in this volume is part of a larger project undertaken in Argentina, Brazil, Chile, Greece, India, the Philippines, and Uruguay.[1]

Purpose of this Chapter

In this introductory chapter we shall briefly review the concern for industrial and economic development in underdeveloped countries; the importance of managerial input in economic development; industrial and economic progress made in Taiwan; strategies of studying the management transfer processes; and the research design utilized for this study.

Concern For Economic Development

Since World War II, economists, sociologists, anthropologists,

[1] Anant R. Negandhi and S. B. Prasad, *Comparative Management* (New York: Appleton-Century-Crofts, 1971).

psychologists, governmental and political leaders, and social workers have turned their attention toward the problems of economic development in underdeveloped countries.

In underdeveloped countries, the quest for economic progress has become the main preoccupation. One author was tempted to call this quest for economic progress "one of the great world crusades of our time."[2] Former Brazilian President Kubitschek seems to have expressed the concern reflected by many leaders of developing countries:

> The majority of our people are convinced that if the road to material progress is barred, Brazil will not be able to avoid the choice between development and the wreckage of its democratic institutions.[3]

Economic Development Strategies

Although many of the growing nations have set forth comprehensive plans for development with specific targets for agricultural, industrial, transportation and social overheads, the main emphasis seems to be on industrialization.

Many economic development theorists would agree that investment is the central key to economic growth. However, in terms of development strategies, there is a wide spectrum of views.

Adler, for example, has argued that although capital formulation ... "is not the whole story [for economic development] ... it is at least half of it and the other half is rather meaningless without it."[4]

Hirschman,[5] on the other hand, stressed the importance of maximizing investment decisions. Galbraith[6] has put emphasis on investment, education, good government, social and economic justice, and a clear sense of purpose. Walinsky[7] and Hagen[8] have stressed the

[2] Murray D. Bryce, *Industrial Development* (New York: McGraw Hill Book Company, Inc., 1960), p. 3.

[3] Claude McMillan, Jr., *et al.*, *International Enterprises in a Developing Economy* (East Lansing, Michigan: Bureau of Business and Economic Research, Michigan State University, 1964), p. 2.

[4] John H. Adler, "Some Policy Problems in Economic Development," *Economic Development and Cultural Change*, Vol. IX, No. 2 (January, 1961), pp. 118-119.

[5] Albert O. Hirschman, *The Strategy of Economic Development* (New Haven: Yale University Press, 1958).

[6] John K. Galbraith, "A Positive Approach to Foreign Aid," *Foreign Affairs*, Vol. 39, No. 3 (April, 1961), pp. 444-457.

[7] Louis J. Walinsky, *Economic Development in Burma, 1951-60* (New York: The Twentieth Century Fund, 1962).

[8] Everett E. Hagen, "How Economic Growth Begins: A General Theory Applied to Japan," *Public Opinion Quarterly*, Vol. XXII, No. 3 (Fall, 1958), pp. 373-383.

importance of entrepreneurial drive and vigor. Sociologists, anthropologists, and psychologists have emphasized the attitudes, cultural traits, perceptions, and personality factors.[9]

Importance of Managerial Input

A close examination of the various theories of economic development would reveal that many economists either assume that "managers" are efficient and capable of implementing the planned industrial projects, or do not give sufficient importance to the "managerial" aspects of the developmental process.

In other words, while economic planning and the issue of resource allocation have received considerable attention from scholars and statesmen alike, the implementation aspect has received very cursory treatment.

We suspect that the real bottleneck in the economic and industrial development process is not a lack of knowledge concerning planning and resource allocation, but rather it is the "managerial" aspect of the development process. This has been recognized increasingly in the last few years.[10] For example, Mr. J. Ross, a leading Chilean executive, recently stated:

> Perhaps it is time to alter our concept of underdevelopment and think in terms of management. This would focus our attention on helping mismanaged areas to improve their organizations and knowledge. No amount of capital investment will succeed in furthering human progress if such wealth producing resources are mishandled or undermined through lack of fundamental concepts.[11]

Management-organization theorist, L. R. Sayles, had this to say: "In the world race for economic growth and for the allegiance and stability of lesser-developed sections of the globe, United States management 'know-how' is a crucial factor."[12] In the same vein,

[9] David McClelland, *The Achieving Society* (New York: D. Van Nostrand Company, 1961).

[10] S. B. Prasad and A. R. Negandhi, *Managerialism For Economic Development* (The Hague: Martinus Nijhoff, 1968).

[11] J. Ross, "The Profit Motive and Its Potential for New Economies," Proceedings, International Management Congress CIOS, XIII (New York: Council for International Progress in Management (U.S.A.) Inc., 1963), Quoted from H. Koontz and C. O'Donnell, *Principles of Management* New York: McGraw Hill Book Company 1968) (4th Edition), p. 764.

[12] Leonard R. Sayles, *Managerial Behavior* (New York: McGraw Hill Book Company, Inc., 1964), p. 17.

Stefan M. Robock said: "If any single factor is the key for unlocking the forces of economic growth in the underdeveloped areas of the world, that factor is management."[13]

The importance of modern management also has been recognized by the Chinese leaders themselves. For example, Si-Chin Kao, then General Manager of the China Productivity and Trade Center, has echoed:

> ... The future development must depend upon a modernized and systematic education ... while modern Western management principles and techniques should be adopted and adapted carefully ... business and industry in the Republic of China must be managed along modern lines. The old-fashioned favoritism, paternalism, and family-centered management must give way to the cold-blooded modern objective and scientific management.[14]

Industrial and Economic Progress in Taiwan[15]

The industrial and economic progress in Taiwan has indeed been impressive during the last 15 years. During this period Taiwan made a transition from her traditional agricultural economy to an industrial one.[16] In specific terms, during the 15-year period between 1953 and 1967 Taiwan's real GNP grew 8.4 per cent per year. This compares very favorably with many of the developed and developing countries. Taiwan's real national income grew by 37.1 per cent between 1957 and 1962, as compared to 3 per cent in Argentina, 32 per cent in Brazil, 17 per cent in Chile, 66 per cent in Japan, 25 per cent in Mexico, and 23 per cent in the United States and India.[17]

Taiwan experienced an average of 14 per cent growth per year in industrial production during the 1953-1967 period. In most of the

[13] Stefan M. Robock, "Management in Underdeveloped Countries," *Advanced Management Journal*, January, 1961, p. 104.

[14] Si-Chin Kao, "Modern Management Development in Taiwan Today," *Industry of Free China*, February, 1969, p. 8.

[15] For details see A. R Negandhi, "New Frontiers for American Business: The Case for Taiwan," *California Management Review*, Vol. XIV, No. 1, Fall 1971, pp. 96-102.

[16] Neil H. Jacoby, U.S. *Aid to Taiwan: A Study of Foreign Aid, Self-Help and Development* (New York: Frederick A. Prager, 1966) especially Chapters VI and VII, pp. 71-102.

[17] A. R. Negandhi, *Private Foreign Investment Climate in India* (East Lansing, Michigan, Graduate School of Business Administration, Division of Research, 1965), pp. 78-101.

developing countries in Asia, Africa, and Latin America the industrial growth has been less than 5 per cent per year.

Indeed, the above indicators of industrial and economic progress pinpoint the envious position of Taiwan among underdeveloped and semi-developed countries in Asia, Africa, and Latin America.

The industrial and economic development process is, however, dynamic and ever changing; it cannot be taken for granted. Even such highly industrialized countries as the United States and West Germany are watchful for their up and downs.

Taiwan's initial progress can be attributed to many factors. Some of the most important among these are:

a. Massive inflow of U.S. capital in terms of economic aid. (Some $1.4 billion during the period of 1951 to 1965.)
b. Constructive governmental economic and industrial policies.
c. A land-reform program and the earlier development of the agricultural sector.
d. An intelligent, hard-working, and well-disciplined labor force.
e. Political stability.
f. The challenge to survive against Communist China.

Many of these resources are not yet fully developed. These resources, coupled with the above factors, may continue to generate economic and industrial expansions in Taiwan.

But the recent economic trends – rising prices and inflation, a shortage of skilled workers, and an abnormal labor turnover in industrial enterprises – pinpoint growing stress in Taiwan's economy. There is increasing concern among economists and responsible governmental officials that Taiwan may slow down or even experience a setback if the appropriate managerial input is not forthcoming in due time. For example, Walter E. Hoadley, Vice-president of the Bank of America, speaking on the future of China's economy expressed:

> Taiwan is losing much of its competitive advantage for low unskilled labor costs ... Taiwan will have to reduce manufacturing inefficiencies, often masked by low-cost labor. Professional management abilities and advanced technology must play increasingly important roles.[18]

T. K. Tusi, a senior economist of CIECD (Council for International Economic Cooperation and Development, Taiwan), in reviewing

[18] Walter E. Hoadley, "The Future of China's Economy," *Kepz Concentrates* (Taiwan), Vol. 3, No. 10 (November, 1968), pp. A-7.

Taiwan's economic growth and future potential, underscored the urgent need for removal of the inefficiencies in industrial and business organizations, and the improvement of methods for training and supplying skilled workers and technical and managerial personnel.[19]

The Purpose of This Study

This brief review of the economic scene in Taiwan combined with the prevailing economic situation in many of the developing countries clearly suggests that, in coming years, the managerial input will play an ever increasing role in generating a higher level of economic and industrial developments in these countries. Thus the main purpose of this study was to specifically explore the feasibility and utility of introducing the more advanced management practices used in developed countries, particularly the United States, to underdeveloped ones.

The Definition of Advanced Management Know-how and Skills

Although many authors have argued for the transfer of managerial practices and skills from developed countries to underdeveloped ones, few have attempted to provide the operational meaning of such terms. For the purpose of this research, we have adopted the definition proposed by AIESBC-International. They have defined managerial skills as "the special capabilities that make a manager what he is. The capacity to collect, process, and evaluate information; the ability to distinguish the alternatives and make a decision; and the resourcefulness in communicating to others the reasons behind his decisions and actions."[20]

Translated into operational terms this may involve the following:

1. Systematic and detailed long-range planning of goals and a means of reaching these goals.
2. Greater involvement of member participants in decision making, both in the planning process and general organizational activities.
3. Objective measurements of achievements against targeted goals.
4. Explanation of deviations between achievements and targeted goals.

[19] T. K. Tusi, "Taiwan's Industrial Growth and Structure," *Industry of Free China*, October, 1968, pp. 21-33.

[20] "International Transfer of Management Skills," *AIESEC International News Letter* (February, 1968), p. 1.

5. Exercising the leadership that will contribute most in increasing employee satisfaction in work and productivity.
6. Establishing selection, training, and promotion procedures which will not only be "equitable and just," but also more conducive to higher productivity.
7. Solicitation of employee cooperation at all levels in achieving the firm's objectives or goals.
8. Utilization of techniques and methods, such as cost accounting, quality control, and budgeting, which will enable the firm to reduce costs.

This list is by no means all inclusive. It only outlines the major facets of managerial practices which are more conducive to higher productivity.

MANAGEMENT TRANSFER PROCESS: RESEARCH STRATEGIES

An examination of pertinent literature suggests many viewpoints from which to study the management transfer process. Among these, the most frequently suggested are:

1. The Study of Transfer Agents[21] such as: (a) The multinational firm; (b) the business school; (c) international technical programs; (d) joint-venture firms in host countries; (e) the expatriate managers from industrially developed countries; (f) foreign educated and trained native managers.

2. The Study of Environmental Context in which firms are operating. The notion here is that socio-cultural, economic, political, and legal factors have considerable impact on management practices and effectiveness and, therefore, the study of such factors will be useful in understanding the management transfer process.

Kamala Chowdhry, for example, at a recent international conference on Social and Cultural Factors in Management Development, observed: "Management subjects, like administrative practices, ... are especially culture-bound and require to be understood in reaction to the social and economic environment of the country."[22]

[21] *The Quarterly Journal of AIESEC International*, Vol. IV, No. 3 and 4, Vol. V No. 1, 1968, 1969.

[22] Kamala Chowdhry, "Social and Cultural Factors in Management Development in India and the Role of Expert," *International Labour Review*, Vol. 94, No. 3 (August, 1966), p. 132.

At the same conference a Japanese Scholar, Shin-Ichi Takezawa, emphasized that "management in essence consists of particularistic responses to given conditions ... and management principles and techniques are conditioned by the demands of socio-cultural environment."[23]

Primarily working on the above notion, Farmer and Richman have provided an elaborate scheme to evaluate environmental conditions in different countries.[24]

The Limitations of these two Approaches

Both of the above methods are useful in increasing our understanding of the management transfer process. However, both of these approaches are limited in scope. A few of these limitations are cited below.

Transfer Agents

The study of transfer agents suffers mainly from the methodological problem of comparing samples and situations. For example, the study of such multi-national firms as Unilever or the Shell Oil Company, by themselves, may suggest a considerable utilization of advanced management practices and know-how. But these firms command considerable resources, both in capital and technological terms, and are larger in size. One has no way of ascertaining the feasibility and relevance of their management know-how and practices for smaller and less technologically oriented local firms in underdeveloped countries.[25]

Similar limitations apply to the study of joint-venture firms, although the problems may be less serious here.

Other transfer agents, such as business schools and technical training programs, are more involved in imparting knowledge about management. However, as Phillipo Perera[26] pointed out, management trans-

[23] Shin-Ichi Takezawa, "Socio-Cultural Aspects of Management in Japan," *International Labour Review*, Vol. 94, No. 3 (August, 1966), p. 147.

[24] R. D. Farmer and B. M. Richman, *Comparative Management and Economic Progress* (Homewood: Richard D. Irwin, 1965).

[25] Wickham Skinner, *American Industry in Developing Economies* (New York: John Wiley and Sons, Inc., 1968).

[26] Phillipo Perara, "Government to Government Assistance: The International Transfer of Management Skills," *The Quarterly Journal of AIESEC International*, Vol. IV, No. 3 (August-October, 1968), p. 31.

fer involves three interrelated components: (a) management knowledge; (b) management skills; and (c) management attitudes.

Management knowledge refers to the tools and fundamentals concerning management discipline; management skills involve the implementation of tools and fundamentals of management; management attitudes refer to the points of view (or perception) of managers concerning managerial tasks and environmental settings. The above agents can and have successfully transferred management knowledge, but at the same time are limited in their ability to transfer managerial skills and attitudes.

Other transfer agents, like expatriate managers and foreign educated local managers, can be somewhat more successful in transferring managerial skills and attitudes. But here again we face the methodological problem of comparing samples and situations. In the first place, managers are few in number and they generally work for large enterprises. Although the case studies of such managers may indeed be very useful in increasing our understanding of the management transfer process, such studies have serious limitations for arriving at any generalizations.

The Study of Environmental Conditions

It would be naive to suggest that societal environments do not affect management practices and effectiveness. However, the actual causal relationships between environmental variables and management practices and effectiveness are difficult to determine. The difficulty can be illustrated by the following statement made by Farmer and Richman who have most ardently advocated the study of environmental contexts for the management transfer process:

> ... The degree of centralization or decentralization of authority depends significantly on literacy level, education, higher education, special management development programs, attitude toward education, view of industrial managers and management, view of authority and subordinates, attitude toward wealth and material gain, view of scientific methods, relevant legal rules, general economic frame work, factors endowment and social overhead capital.[27]

The above proposition suggests a causal relationship between twenty or more independent variables and the distribution of authority in

[27] Farmer and Richman, *op. cit.*, p. 38.

organizations. Thus, in trying to say so much about causal relationships between these two variables, the authors end up saying very little which increases our understanding of the management transfer process.[28]

In other words, as Schollhammer has aptly remarked:

> The emphasis on environmental conditions has the effect that the individual enterprise is regarded as being basically a passive creature of external constraints. As a result, there is generally an overemphasis on the necessity for environmental adaption and not enough attention is paid to the fact that management may choose to act in defiance of certain external conditions.[29]

In the same vein, Boddewyn has argued that "A real danger exists ... of letting the environment crowd out the comparative analysis .... Comparisons are somewhat precariously balanced between management itself and its environment."[30] One needs, therefore, he adds, to "take care not to throw out the management baby with environmental bath or smother it in a blanket of social context."[31]

RESEARCH DESIGN OF THIS STUDY

Realizing the various limitations of the above methods, we attempted to study the management transfer process through empirical investigation of management practices and the effectiveness of American subsidiaries and comparable (in terms of size, technology product-mix, etc.) local firms in developing countries. Our rationale in using this approach is as follows.

Many researchers working in the area of international management have found that American subsidiaries are more progressive in their management practices and are able to achieve higher effectiveness. Kannappan and Burgess, for example, commenting on the performance of American subsidiaries abroad, had this to say:

> These firms stand out in their orientations toward modern industry and dynamic internal management policies. They are generally rated high in

[28] Hans Schollhammer, "The Comparative Management Theory Jungle," *Academy of Management Journal*, Vol. 12, No. 1 (March, 1969), pp. 86-89.

[29] *Ibid.*, pp. 86-87.

[30] Jean Boddewyn, "Comparative Concepts in Management, Administration and Organization" (Memmo. Draft), p. 12.

[31] *Ibid.*

technical competence, quality of product, and managerial skill and are regarded as farsighted in recruiting the best personnel, in providing the best salaries and working conditions, and in delegating authority.[32]

Among others, Dunning[33] found that the U.S. subsidiaries in Britain were more progressive in their management practices and showed higher growth and profitability than the comparable local British firms. *The American Challenge*, by Servan-Schreiber,[34] echoed the same contention.

American subsidiaries abroad are in the advantageous position of knowing advanced management practices through their parent companies in the United States; as such, they are more likely to utilize these management practices in their overseas operations.

We feel that study of such firms will determine the feasibility of transferring management skills and know-how within a given environmental context. Meanwhile, the examination of management practices and effectiveness in comparable local firms will indicate the actual differences between *what is feasible* and *what is not being done*, but could be done, in a specific developing country. We believe that, with this knowledge, one is in a better position to inquire into the environmental impact on management practices and effectiveness and thus, the management transfer process.

As stated earlier, the Taiwan study reported in this volume is part of a larger project undertaken in Argentina, Brazil, Chile, Greece, India, the Philippines, and Uruguay. We studied American subsidiaries and comparable local firms in each of these countries. In Taiwan, however, we included the Japanese subsidiaries in our sample, along with American subsidiaries and the comparable local firms. It is believed that not only the American subsidiaries, but also other firms from the relatively developed countries (Western European countries and Japan, for example) might have undergone adaptive processes. Their experiences may well be relevant and useful to the firms in lesser

[32] S. Kannappan and E. Burgess, *Business Performance Abroad: A Case Study of Aluminum Limited in India* (Washington: National Planning Association, 1962), p. 25.

[33] John H. Dunning, *American Investment in British Manufacturing Industry* (London: George Allen and Unwin, Ltd., 1958) also see "U.S. Subsidiaries in Britain and Their U.K. Competitors," *Business Ratios* (London), No. 1 (Autumn, 1966), pp. 5-18.

[34] Servan-Schreiber J. J., *The American Challenge* (New York: Atheneum Publishers, 1968).

developed countries. Such a belief was expressed in our own writings,[35] as well as in the recent "International Conference on Management Development for the Developing Countries and the Relevance of European Experience" held in Palermo, Italy, in June of 1969.

To an extent, this three-way comparison can be typified as (a) the "ideal" type (U.S. subsidiary) (b) the "advanced-neighbor" type (Japanese subsidiary), and (c) the emerging, aspiring, and traditional local type.

Method and Sample

Both personal interviews and questionnaire methods were used to collect necessary data in Taiwan. Structured and non-structured interview techniques were employed to solicit information. A 40-page interview guide, prepared for this purpose, is reproduced in Appendix A. On an average, we interviewed 8 to 10 executives and 8 to 10 supervisory and blue-collar workers in each company studied.

Interview Sample

A total of 27 firms were investigated through intensive interview techniques. Of these, nine were American subsidiaries, seven were Japanese subsidiaries, and eleven were local firms in Taiwan. The size and industrial classification of these firms are given in Tables 1-1 and 1-2.

Each American subsidiary was paired with a Japanese subsidiary and local firm on the basis of product-mix, technology (hardware used),

TABLE 1-1. *Number of Employees in Companies Studied (Interview Sample)*

Number of Employees	U.S. Subsidiary	Local Company	Japanese Subsidiary
100 to 500	7	6	3
501 to 2000	1	4	3
2001 to 3000	1	1	1
3000 and more			
TOTAL	9	11	7

[35] Prasad-Negandhi, *op. cit.*

TABLE 1-2. *Industrial Classification of Companies Studied (Interview Sample)*

Type of Principal Activity	U.S. Subsidiary	Local Company	Japanese Subsidiary
Chemical and Pharmaceutical	5	6	4
Petroleum			
Light Enginerring Products	1	2	2
Heavy Engineering Products			
Electrical-Consumer; Nondurable Goods		1	
Electrical-Consumer; Durable and Industrial Goods	3	2	1
Rubber Tires			
Soaps and Cosmetics			
Soft Drinks, Canned Products			
TOTAL	9	11	7

and number of employees. To provide some perspective of management practices in the U.S. parent companies, we also studied 15 of these companies in the U.S.A.

Questionnaire Sample

A questionnaire survey was conducted among the 300 industrial firms in Taiwan to solicit information concerning their attitudes and viewpoints about important management practices. Of these 300 firms, 99 returned usable questionnaires (23 U.S. subsidiaries and 76 local firms). This questionnaire is reproduced in Appendix B.

ELEMENTS OF MANAGEMENT PRACTICES AND MANAGEMENT EFFECTIVENESS INVESTIGATED

Management Practices

1. Planning
   a. Planning objectives
   b. The nature and scope of planning

	c. Time-horizons in planning d. The resultant plans e. Reviews of plans f. Participation and information-sharing in planning
2. Organization	a. Authority-responsibility relationship b. Organization charts c. Degree of centralization and decentralization d. Degree of specialization e. The use of informal organizations and management attitudes toward such groups f. Grouping of activities and departments g. Use of specialist staff and their relationship with line executives
3. Manpower Management	a. Methods used in appraising, selecting, and training personnel b. Promotion criteria used c. Management development practices used d. Compensation practices
4. Direction and Leadership	a. The techniques used for motivating highlevel man-power to cooperate in achieving organizational objectives and goals b. The methods and techniques used for motivating workers c. Supervisory techniques used d. Leadership style used

5. Control
   a. Control techniques used for different areas, i.e., finance, production, marketing, etc.
   b. Types of control standards
   c. Information feedback systems and procedures for corrective actions

Management Effectiveness

1. Management ability to attract and retain high-level manpower
2. Employee morale and satisfaction in work
3. Employee turnover and absenteeism
4. Interpersonal relationships in organizational settings
5. Subsystem behavioral relationships (Departmental relationships)
6. The executive's perception of the firm's overall objectives
7. Utilization of high-level manpower
8. Organizational effectiveness in adapting to the external environments

Enterprise Effectiveness

1. Return on sales and on investment
2. Growth in market share
3. Increase in sales
4. Growth in price of stock and P/E ratio
5. Unit cost
6. Utilization of plant facilities
7. Scrap loss

Organization of the Book

The book is organized to provide comparative perspectives of management practices and effectiveness in American subsidiaries, Japanese subsidiaries, and local firms in Taiwan. In the beginning of each chapter we attempt to highlight the management practices of American firms in the United States. Information concerning various management practices in these firms was obtained through our own study of 15 U.S. parent companies and studies of American firms by other researchers.

At the end of each chapter, we endeavor to provide international comparisons. These data are derived from our larger project reported elsewhere.[36]

Although we inquire about the fundamental question of the feasibility in transferring specific advanced management practices to Taiwan throughout this volume, the overall question is taken up in Chapter 8. This chapter also provides a brief summary of our findings in Taiwan. Because of the nature of the research involved (the small sample size), comparative frequency statistics are presented rather than statistical analyses of data. These may be seen in various tables in Chapter 2 through 7. In Chapter 8, however, we have attempted to carry out more rigorous statistical analyses of data.

What Follows?

In the next chapter we begin our analysis of management practices in American and Japanese subsidiaries and local firms by inquiring about their planning orientations. Here such issues as planning objectives, the nature and scope of planning, time horizons in planning, frequency of reviewing plans, and participation and information-sharing in the planning process are explored.

Chapter 3 discusses the policy-making and control mechanisms used by the firms studied. Specific data collected and analyzed in this chapter are: (a) the nature and scope of policy-making; (b) standard-settings for blue-collar employees and clerical employees; (c) cost and budgetary controls; (d) quality control; (e) time and motion study; (f) equipment maintenance; and (g) return on investment and other financial controls used.

Chapter 4 deals with the organizational aspect. This chapter analyzes such topics as grouping of activities, layers of hierarchy, authority definition, delegation of authority, degree of decentralization in decision-making, uses of committees, and executive attitudes toward decentralization.

Chapter 5 examines the leadership styles and practices found among firms in Taiwan.

Chapter 6 concerns manpower management practices. Here, manpower policies as well as various personnel practices are analyzed.

[36] Negandhi-Prasad *op. cit.*

This chapter also concludes our analysis of management practices observed in the three sets of firms in Taiwan.

Chapter 7 takes up the issue of managerial effectiveness in industrial firms in Taiwan. Data concerning various behavioral and economic criteria of effectiveness are analyzed.

As stated earlier, Chapter 8 attempts to deal directly with the fundamental question of feasibility and utility of transferring advanced management practices into industrial enterprises in Taiwan. Preceeding the exploration of this question, a brief summary of our findings is provided.

CHAPTER II

LONG-RANGE PLANNING

Introduction

The purpose of this chapter is to analyze the planning orientations of the companies studied. In discussing this topic, our concern will be more on the nature and type of planning rather than on the procedure, process, and methodology of planning activities.

Specifically, data were collected for the following items:

1. Planning objectives (why do companies plan?)
2. The nature and scope of planning
3. Time-horizons in planning
4. The resultant plans
5. Reviews of plans
6. Participation and information-sharing in planning.

In analyzing these data, we shall compare and contrast American subsidiaries, Japanese subsidiaries, and local Taiwan firms. Also, wherever possible, comparative data from other countries is provided. Preceding the analysis of data, however, we will briefly review the practices of American companies in the United States.

Planning Concept

Planning is the most important and basic function of management. Henry Fayol, the father of management thought, puts planning first: "To administer is to plan, organize, command, coordinate, and control." [1]

As Koontz and O'Donnell have remarked, "Planning involves selection of enterprise and departmental objectives and goals as well

[1] Henry Fayol *General and Industrial Management* (New York: Pitman Publishing Corporatiou, 1949).

as determination of the means of reaching them."[2] In other words, "Planning is deciding in advance what to do, how to do it, when to do it, and who is to do it. Planning bridges the gap from where we are to where we want to go. It makes it possible for things to occur which would not otherwise happen."[3]

Planning is considered a prerequisite to the company's growth and profitability. The Stanford Research Institute, for example, found that "in the case of both high growth and low-growth companies, those that now support planning programs have shown a superior growth rate in recent years."[4]

Although long-range planning has become an accepted practice in many U.S. companies, the concept of long-range planning means different things to different people. It is, therefore, necessary to define this concept at the outset.

George A. Steiner has defined long-range planning thus:

> "Long-range planning deals with the futurity of present decisions in terms of setting goals, developing strategies to achieve them, translating strategies into detailed operational programs, and assuring that plans are carried out."[5 and 6]

Scott has defined planning in terms of the process of decision making. "Planning is an analytical process which encompasses an assessment of the future, the determination of desired objectives in the context of that future, the development of alternative courses of action to achieve such objectives, and selection of a course or courses of action from among these alternatives."[7]

[2] Harold Koontz and Cyril O'Donnell, *Principles of Management* (New York: McGraw-Hill Book Company, 3rd ed., 1964), p. 69.

[3] *Ibid.*, p. 71.

[4] Quoted from George A. Steiner, "Does Planning Pay Off?," *California Management Review*, Vol. V, No. 2 (Winter, 1962), p. 37.

[5] George A. Steiner, ed., *Managerial Long-Range Planning* (New York: McGraw-Hill Book Company, 1963), p. 312.

[6] George A. Steiner and W. M. Cannon, ed., *Multinational Corporate Planning* (New York: MacMillan Company, 1966), pp. 8-16.

[7] B. Scott, *Long Range Planning in American Industry* (New York: American Management Association, 1965), p. 21.

PLANNING ORIENTATIONS OF THE AMERICAN COMPANIES IN THE U.S.

Planning Practices of the 15 U.S. Parent Companies

Data on planning practices of the American companies suggest a strong trend toward systematic and comprehensive long-range planning. For example, our research with the 15 U.S. parent companies indicates that the large majority (13) undertake comprehensive planning involving all major activities such as finance, marketing and sales, production, plant capacity and equipment, organization, and manpower. The planning cycle is for durations ranging from five to ten years. The resulting plans are detailed and systematic. Plans are reviewed and revised, if necessary, on a quarterly and yearly basis. All levels of line and staff managers participate in the planning process.

Findings of other researchers in the United States correspond to the actual planning practices of these 15 U.S. parent companies surveyed by us.

Holden, Pederson and Germane's recent study of 15 large-scale U.S. companies, for example, indicates that foreward planning is an accepted practice in all firms. The following excerpt summarizes their findings:

> Although a five-year planning cycle is the prevailing pattern, some notable exceptions are found. ... Companies that have had successful experience in long-range planning and that are cognizant of the need to extend the cycle for certain elements are either moving rapidly to a ten-year program or are giving serious consideration to that eventuality ... In contrast to early corporate planning, the current practice is to develop comprehensive projections involving productline, sales, facilities, research and development, manpower, organization, structure and ... finance. ... The involvement of line management from bottom to top in the planning process is general practice ... (and) Chief executives devote from 25 to 70 per cent of their time to long-range planning.[8]

A conference held at U.C.L.A. in 1962, to discuss long-range planning practices of large U.S. companies and governmental agencies, suggests the following trends:[9]

[8] P. E. Holden, C. A. Pederson and G. E. Germane, *Top Management* (New York: McGraw-Hill Book Company, 1968), p. 3-4.

[9] The following companies and governmental agencies were represented at the conference: (1) Aerojet-General Corporation; (2) All State Ins., Co., (3) American

a. Long-range planning is an integral part of the operations in all organizations which participated in the conference.
b. A number of companies and agencies represented at the conference have rather detailed five-year planning programs. In some instances, coordinated strategic plans are made within a ten-year time frame in addition to detailed five-year plans.
c. Strategic plans in the ten-year time span are sometimes revised annually and sometimes only as need seems to indicate. Five-year plans usually are revised annually and extended one year in time.
d. Plans cover the following major activities of the company: Production, manpower, finance, management, personnel, sales, industrial relations, organization, marketing, public relations, diversification and research and development.
e. Structurally, three sets of plans are made: (1) strategic long-range plans; (2) intermediate-range five-year plans; (3) operational plans.
f. A committee of top managers in the functional areas assures proper planning coordination. The primary responsibility for planning rests with those responsible with operations.[10]

To be sure, formal comprehensive planning is comparatively new even among American companies. As the recent research of Ringbakk[11] indicates, formal long-range planning is mainly nothing more than "ivory tower" planning by staff members to whom line managers are unwilling to commit themselves. Nevertheless, as the above findings suggest, a large majority of American firms do plan ahead for at least a five-year period.

PLANNING ORIENTATIONS OF THE U.S. AND JAPANESE SUBSIDIARIES AND LOCAL TAIWAN FIRMS

Table 2-1 reports data on five aspects of planning: 1) planning objectives; 2) nature of planning; 3) length of planning; 4) resulting plans; and 5) frequency of reviewing plans.

Airlines; (4) Atomic Energy Commission; (5) North American Aviation; (6) Bendix Corporation; (7) Continental Oil Co.; (8) U.S. Department of Defense; (9) Federal Aviation Agency; (10) Ford Motor Company; (11) Glendale Federal Savings; (12) International Machine Corp.; (13) Lockheed Aircraft Corp.; (14) National Aeronautics and Space Administration; (15) Southern California Edison Company; (16) Standard Oil Co.

[10] See George A. Steiner (ed.), *Managerial Long-Range Planning*, *op. cit.*, pp. 311-326.

[11] Kjell-Anne Ringbakk, *Organized Corporate Planning Systems: An Empirical Study of Planning Practices and Experience in American Big Business*, unpublished Ph.D. dissertation, University of Washington, 1968.

Planning Objectives

Why do companies plan? Responses from companies studied indicate that the firms' objectives in undertaking long-range planning are guided by two major considerations; long-term growth and higher profitability.

Nature of Planning and Resulting Plans

Our inquiry concerning the nature of planning and resulting plans in the three sets of companies indicates that the American subsidiaries take considerable care in this area. As data in Table 2-1 show, seven out of nine American subsidiaries undertake comprehensive planning which involves financial, product, plant, and manpower aspects. The resulting plans of these companies are detailed and cover extensive forecasts on many facets of their operations. Particularly, five of the nine U.S. subsidiaries undertake planning in almost the same way as their parent companies in the United States.

Also, in the results of a questionnaire survey, 60 per cent of the American subsidiaries state that their planning is closely related to the parent companies' practices.

In contrast to the American subsidiaries, only a little more than one-half of the local companies (6 out of 11) undertake some sort of planning, and the rest does not plan ahead. Of these six local companies, only three have prepared detailed plans.

Japanese subsidiaries are more like local firms in their planning orientations. Although four of the seven companies undertake some planning, and the rest at least do formal planning for product-mix or financial budgeting, their plans are sketchy and less detailed. As the manager of a Japanese subsidiary explains, "Our plans are in our heads ... we know where we would like to go ... but our employees do not know exactly what we have in mind." Both the local firms and the Japanese subsidiaries share this belief or strategy.

Similar conclusions are drawn by Yoshino in his study of Japanese firms in Japan. Yoshino,[12] for example, has argued that it is the *ringi* system of decision-making practiced by the Japanese enterprises which discourages long-range planning. Under this system of decision-making, authority and responsibilities for each level of management

[12] M. Y. Yoshino, *Japan's Managerial System* (Cambridge: The MIT Press, 1968).

TABLE 2-1. *Planning Orientations of the U.S. and Japanese Subsidiaries and Local Firms in Taiwan*

Planning Orientation	U.S. Subsidiary (n = 9)	Japanese Subsidiary (n = 7)	Local Firm (n = 11)
1. Planning Objectives (*Why does the company plan?*)			
a. For long-term growth	5	3	4
b. For higher profitability	4	4	4
c. No-specific objectives			3
2. Nature of Planning			
a. Comprehensive- (Financial, product, plant, manpower, etc.)	7	4	6
b. Product planning only		1	
c. Financial budgeting only	2	2	
d. Random or no formal planning			5
3. Length of Planning			
a. Five years or more	4	3	4
b. One or two years	5	4	2
c. Ad hoc – no formal planning			5
4. Resulting Plans			
a. Detailed plans and extensive forecasts	5	2	3
b. Limited plants and forecasts	4	3	3
c. Random forecasts only		2	5
5. Frequency of Reviews			
a. Monthly and quarterly	6	1	1
b. Semi-annually		2	2
c. Yearly		2	
d. As and when required	3	2	8

are not clearly defined. No policy guidelines are specified by top management. And there is no "... company-wide planning. It was, rather, a piecemeal approach to decision-making, with each proposal being examined not against a master plan or company-wide objectives, but on a case-by-case basis."[13]

Length of Planning

As we saw earlier among the American companies in the United States, the five-year planning period seems quite common. This trend is only somewhat visible in the case of companies in Taiwan. For example, four of the nine American subsidiaries plan for a five-year period and the remaining five undertake planning for only a one-year period. Almost a similar proportion of Japanese subsidiaries do the same. In the case of local firms, those companies which undertake planning favor a five-year period. Four of these six companies plan for such a period.

Review of Plans

A company's concern for future planning can also be discerned by looking at its review procedure. Here we also find that the American subsidiaries are more serious about their planning. For example, six out of nine American subsidiaries review their plans monthly and quarterly. In contrast to this, the majority of the local firms review their plans on an ad-hoc basis.

Participation and Information-Sharing in the Planning Process

Needles to say, the success of the firm's planning largely depends upon those who implement it. As Ringbakk has demonstrated, "ivory tower" planning by a specialized staff department, without the involvement of line and lower-level managers, is bound to suffer in its implementations. This is why the Holden, Pederson, Germane study indicates that successful companies tend to involve all levels of managers in their planning process.

Looking at the situation in Taiwan, however, we get a somewhat disturbing picture. By and large, the Japanese and local companies are secretive about their planning. Many of their senior and middle level executives do not know about the companies' future plans.

[13] *Ibid.*, p. 263.

TABLE 2-2. *Participation and Information-Sharing in the Planning Process*

Participation and Information-Sharing	U.S. Subsidiary (n = 9)	Japanese Subsidiary (n = 7)	Local Firm (n = 11)
1. Participation in Planning			
a. Chief executive/ owner only	2	7	8
b. Top level and middle executives	7		3
c. All levels of managers			
2. Information-Sharing			
a. Confidential memos/ verbal reports	2	4	6
b. Special reports-circulated restrictively	4	3	5
c. General reports-circulated widely	3		

However, American subsidiaries practice an "open door" policy and encourage their employees to participate in the planning process. This can easily be seen from the data presented in Table 2-2. As we saw earlier, similar inference is drawn by Yoshino[14] with respect to companies in Japan.

International Comparisons

Data in Table 2-3 provide international comparisons on two aspects of the planning function: (1) length of planning, and (2) the nature and scope of planning. These data were collected from the American subsidiaries and local firms in the five developing countries, namely: Argentina, Brazil, India, the Philippines, and Uruguay. In all, 92 firms were investigated, of which 47 were American subsidiaries, and 45 were comparable local firms.

As can be seen from this table, a much larger proportion of the U.S. subsidiaries in these five developing countries (73 per cent) undertake long-range planning of five years' duration. However, there are no appreciable differences in the nature and scope of planning

[14] *Ibid.*, pp. 254-272.

undertaken by the U.S. subsidiaries in Taiwan and other developing countries.

There are no substantial differences between the planning orientations of the local companies in these five developing countries and the local firms in Taiwan. That is, by and large, local companies tend to place more emphasis on short-range planning (one or two-year duration). Their plans are less systematic and detailed than those of the U.S. subsidiaries in the countries. However, as data in Table 2-3 show, about 45 per cent of the local companies in India and the Philippines undertake long-range planning, and 40 per cent of the firms studied develop plans which are comparable to those of the U.S. subsidiaries. In this manner, both the local companies and the Japanese subsidiaries in Taiwan are more like the local companies in India and the Philippines than those in the Latin American countries.

Environmental Factors Affecting Planning

The question which remains to be answered is: "why are the local companies in developing countries less concerned with long-range planning"? Is it because of their socio-economic, political, legal, and cultural environments? We do not pretend to have a final answer to this important question. Our initial inquiry with the executives of the companies studied, revealed the following:

A large majority of the executives interviewed (58 per cent, n = 570) in Argentina, Brazil, India, the Philippines, and Uruguay indicated that the seller's market conditions in those countries make planning less necessary for achieving higher profitability. In this market situation, all firms are making high profits, regardless of their managerial practices. More or less the same proportion of executives (56 per cent) pointed out the governmental control on prices and the scarcity of raw materials are inhibiting factors in undertaking long-range planning. Inflation, political situations, and governmental attitudes toward the business community are mentioned as additional factors which discourage firms from planning for the future. Detailed data are presented in Table 2-4.

TABLE 2-3. *International Comparisons of Planning Orientations*

Planning Orientation	Argentina, Brazil, Uruguay*		India*		The Philippines*		Taiwan**		
	U.S.	Local	U.S.	Local	U.S.	Local	U.S.	Japanese	Local
Length of Planning									
a. Five years or more	15	1	12	6	6	7	4	3	4
b. One or two years	3	7	4	8	2	4	5	4	2
c. Ad-hoc	2	9	1	3	2	–	–	–	5
Total	20	17	17	17	10	11	9	7	11
Nature of Planning									
a. Comprehensive and systematic	10	–	8	6	6	5	5	2	3
b. Systematic, but limited	4	9	5	6	2	2	4	3	3
c. Ad-hoc randomly done	6	8	4	5	2	4	–	2	5
Total	20	17	17	17	10	11	9	7	11

* Data for Argentina, Brazil, India, the Philippines, and Uruguay are reproduced from A. R. Negandhi and S. B. Prasad, *Comparative Management*, (New York: Appleton-Century-Crofts, 1971), pp. 45-47. Permission of the publisher is gratefully acknowledged.

** Data from Table 2-1 "Resulting Plans."

TABLE 2-4. *Impact of Environmental Variables on Long-Range Planning Practices in the Five Underdeveloped Countries (Interview Responses*)*

Environmental Variables	Argentina (N=65)	Brazil (N=90)	India (N=272)	Philippines (N=77)	Uruguay (N=66)	Total (N=570)
1. Nature of competition (Seller's vs. Buyer's Market)	30 (46)	47 (52)	180 (66)	38 (49)	35 (53)	330 (58)
2. Nature of the economic situation (Inflation)	45 (69)	75 (83)	90 (33)	48 (62)	40 (67)	298 (52)
3. Governmental control on prices and the availability of raw materials	20 (31)	32 (36)	210 (77)	30 (39)	25 (38)	317 (56)
4. Political situation	40 (62)	50 (56)	32 (12)	10 (13)	30 (45)	162 (28)
5. Governmental attitude toward busines community	22 (34)	35 (39)	45 (17)	20 (25)	26 (39)	148 (26)

– Reproduced from A. R. Negandhi and S. B. Prasad *Comparative Management* (New York: Appleton-Century-Crofts, 1971), p. 174. Permission of the publisher is gratefully acknowledged.

* Respondents included the senior and middle-level executives of the companies studied.

+ Figures in parentheses show the percentage of all respondents. Many respondents mentioned more than one factor, therefore, figures are not strictly additive.

Concern in Taiwan

Similar interviews with executives in Taiwan suggest the following factors as inhibiting forces in undertaking long-range planning:

Factors Affecting Long-Range Planning in Taiwan	*Percentage of the Total Respondents (n = 27)
a. Stiff competition	63%
b. Govt. controls on prices and the unavailability of raw materials	37%
c. Political situation	4%

* Percentage does not add up to 100% because the respondents mentioned more than one factor.

It is interesting to note that while the executives in the other five developing countries blame the seller's market condition, their counterparts in Taiwan pronounce stiff competition as the main obstacle for future planning. This contradictory evidence, or so it seems on the surface, does represent the real condition in those countries.

In the case of Taiwan, as we saw in Chapter 1, the industrial and economic progress has been phenomenal. Real income, for example, has increased three-fold during the 15-year period of 1952-1967. The per capita income, as well as the real wages during the same period, has doubled. The total employment has expanded from 2.9 million in 1952 to 3.9 million in 1966.

Of course, this increase in "affluence" has created a greater purchasing power in the hands of consumers. To keep up with increasing demand, the production of goods and services has gone up four to six fold. For example, since 1952, on average, three factories per day have gone up in Taiwan.

Although in recent years the Taiwan consumer has greatly increased his assortment of goods and services, he still remains unsophisticated in differentiating qualities of goods and services. In other words, the main yardstick of comparison utilized by the typical Taiwan consumer is price; and, accordingly, the competition has been waged on a price basis. The constant cutting of prices to beat the competition has become an accepted practice of many small and medium-size local firms in Taiwan. This reduction in prices, coupled with the increase in wages without proportional gain through higher productivity, has reduced the surplus or profit margins of many firms. The shrinking profits have made it difficult for many local firms to introduce, or even think of introducing, advanced management practices. So, in a manner of speaking, many local firms "run scared" of losing out in the prevailing competitive forces in Taiwan. Surprisingly enough, these firms are not scared of the "big boys", namely the U.S. and Japanese subsidiaries and the larger local firms, but rather seem to be concerned with the so-called "backyard entrepreneurs" whose factories are generally one-man operations.[15] Many of the executives interviewed

[15] Of course, small manufacturers can beat the larger ones by price competition, by not confirming to governmental regulations with respect to factory security measures, hiring conditions, and minimum wages. (I am most thankful to Professor Lamp Li for drawing my attention to this fact.)

in Taiwan refer to this type of competitive situation which, in their opinion, affects the future planning functions of their firms.

The general manager of a medium-size local pharmaceutical firm echoed the concern of many in these words:

> We copy as many products as possible by looking at the U.S. magazines, newspapers, medical journals, etc. This is our way of getting somewhere in this competitive world ... we also reduce prices of our products to meet the competition from the small manufacturers. Big American companies do not bother us as their prices are very high and they aimed to enter a rich man's market. We like to concentrate on middle and poor class markets ... what worries us, is the small manufacturer ... as he may be selling at the cost or even below cost ... to meet this competition, we reduce our prices which leaves very little profit to introduce any necessary changes in our management practices.

In the case of the other five developing countries, although per capita income has been increasing, the supply of goods and services lags behind. This, in turn, creates a seller's market condition in all of these countries. Many executives interviewed in these five countries – Argentina, Brazil, India, the Philippines, and Uruguay – admit that they have no incentive to undertake long-range planning, and for that matter, to utilize any advanced management practices, as long as they are harvesting huge profits due to seller's market conditions.

Notwithstanding the above environmental constraints which may discourage long-range planning, it is interesting to note that none of the executives in any of the six developing countries mentioned the socio-cultural factors which affect the planning function. In other words, factors mentioned by those executives are mainly economic and governmental. These factors are, to a great extent, "man-made" and not necessarily rooted in the cultural heritage of a society. If this is so, then one has reason to believe that planning practices are transferable from more developed countries to developing countries. The empirical data from the six developing countries support this contention. For example, taking the six countries as a group, we find that approximately 40 to 45 per cent of the local companies studied were able to undertake long-range planning in a systematic manner. This proportion was even higher among the U.S. subsidiaries operating in those countries.

Planning is closely related to two of the basic functions of management: Policy-making and controlling. In the next chapter we will analyze these managerial functions as practiced in Taiwan.

CHAPTER III

POLICY-MAKING AND CONTROL MECHANISM

Introduction

The managerial function of control assumes an important role in achieving organizational objectives and planned goals. Control function is closely related to both planning and organizational structure. In other words, as Chaple and Sayles have pointed out:

> Controls are a basic element in the structure of any organization, whether it is private or governmental. They provide a primary incentive and indicate where the individual members of the organization should apply their energies. Most important, they are the signal that should bring into action one or more of the supervisory techniques ... and perhaps staff activities. Without adequate controls to direct managerial efforts, time and energy are wasted, and potential crises are ignored while smoothly functioning activities received needles attention ... controls are the most important means to detect organizational defects ... they are the essential bridge between the organization structure and administrative behavior.[1]

There are various control devices available to managers of modern business organizations. The most basic controlling devices used by many corporations are policy guidelines. As Holden *et al.* has stated, "Corporate policies, when thoughtfully conceived and properly promulated, constitute one of the most effective instruments of overall control."[2]

Some of the other more important control techniques frequently used by the industrial enterprises are: (a) cost controls; (b) budgeting; (c) management audit; (d) profit and loss statement; (e) return on investment; and (f) statistical quality control.

[1] E. D. Chaple and L. R. Sayles, *The Measure of Management* (New York: McGraw-Hill Book Company, 1961), p. 78.

[2] P. E. Holden, *et al.*, *Top Management* (New York: McGraw-Hill Book Co., 1968), p. 27.

The purpose of this chapter is to discuss control practices and devices utilized by American and Japanese subsidiaries and local firms in Taiwan. Specifically, data on the following items were collected:

1. Nature and scope of policy-making
2. Standard-setting for producing goods and services, blue-collar workers, clerical employees, and supervisory personnel
3. Cost control
4. Budgetary control
5. Quality control
6. Time and motion studies
7. Equipment maintenance
8. Return on investment
9. Profit and loss statement
10. Management audit

Preceding the analysis of data collected in Taiwan, we shall provide a comparative perspective by briefly reviewing the control practices and techniques utilized by U.S. parent companies and other American companies in the United States.

CONTROL PRACTICES OF MAJOR U.S. COMPANIES

Major Policies

Data collected from the 15 U.S. parent companies indicate that the large majority of these companies stress policy-formulation and utilize policy-guidelines as overall control measures. For example, of the 15 companies, 14 have documented policies and 12 of these firms have special policy-committees to formulate, document, and communicate major policies of the firm. Generally speaking, such policies deal with relationships with the following important agents: consumers, suppliers, competitors, union, government, and community.

Although policies are made by either the policy-committee or top executives themselves, senior and middle-level executives are encouraged to participate in the discussion of formulating policies and devising guidelines for their implementations. In other words, these policies are neither "ivory tower" nor authoritarian in nature. Most of the executives we interviewed indicate a sense of involvement in arriving at these policies.

Other Control Techniques Used

These parent companies also provide formal policy statements concerning major functional areas such as production, marketing, finance, distribution, purchasing, personnel recruitment, and promotion. In most of these functional areas, performance standards are firmly set and every attempt is made to adhere to these pre-set standards.

Among many other controlling measures, cost and budgetary controls, profit and loss statements, return on investment, periodical management audit, time and motion studies, statistical quality control, and inventory control are standard measures utilized by the U.S. parent companies studied. Holden, Pederson and Germane, in their study of 15 large-scale U.S. companies, also found similar types of control devices used by these companies.[3]

CONTROL MEASURES USED BY COMPANIES IN TAIWAN

Major and Functional Policies

Three aspects of policy-making in the U.S. and Japanese subsidiaries and local firms in Taiwan are reported in Table 3-1: (a) documentation of major and functional areas policies; (b) participation in policy-formulation; and (c) review of policies.

Data suggests that, by and large, the U.S. subsidiaries follow the practices of their parent companies in documenting policies and communicating with their employees. For example, five of the nine U.S. subsidiaries formally state their major policies and product-line policies; four of them also spell out their marketing and manpower policies. The fact that U.S. subsidiaries in Taiwan closely follow the practices of their parent companies was also borne out in our questionnaire survey. In answering the question: "To what extent does the overall management policy of your company depend on your parent company," approximately 53 per cent of the respondents (n = 23) suggest that their policies are largely built around the policies of their parent companies. While 41 per cent indicated that their policies are moderately closer to the policies of their parent companies, only 6 per cent of those who responded felt no impact of policies of parent companies. In contrast to the U.S. subsidiaries, the Japanese subsidiaries are quite diffused about their major and functional area policies. Only one

[3] *Ibid.*, especially pp. 22-36.

out of seven of these companies formally states its major policies; two subsidiaries outline only marketing and product line policies.

The local firms are closer to Japanese firms than American firms. Only less than one-third (3 out of 11) have documented policies, while the rest operate on an ad-hoc basis. However, the three progressive local firms which do spell out their policies, are quite thorough in their undertakings.

Specific Areas of Concern

Our inquiry into the areas of concern among the companies surveyed by questionnaire suggests the following trend:

Of the 23 American subsidiaries responding, more than two-thirds attach importance to pricing, personnel selection, plant investment, salary and wages, and control aspects.

Among the local firms, approximately two-thirds of the companies (n = 76) show concern for personnel selection and plant investment, while more than one-half of those responding are concerned about product-line, borrowing and control aspects.

The detailed results of this inquiry are presented in Table 3-2.

It is interesting to note from these data that such factors as employee training, employee relations, purchasing, acquisition, and expansion are considered much less important. Less than one-third of the companies surveyed seemed to be concerned enough to have specific policies in these areas.

Although personnel selection and control aspects are viewed as important factors by both the U.S. subsidiaries and the local firms, their policies and practices are not necessarily the same. As we will see in Chapter 6, they differ considerably both in their orientations and specific practices in these areas.

Participation in Policy-Formulation

As we noted earlier, in the U.S. parent companies policies are mainly formulated by the policy committee, and there is a greater consultation with senior and middle-level executives in formulating the policies. The available empirical evidence suggests that the policy implementation is more effective when there is a broader participation in the formulation of policies. Filley and House,[4] for example, have recently

[4] Alan C. Filley and Robert J. House, *Managerial Process and Organizational*

TABLE 3-1. *Major and Functional Policy-Making in Companies in Taiwan*

Major and Functional Policies	U.S. Subsidiary (n = 9)	Japanese Subsidiary (n = 7)	Local Firm (n = 11)
Major Policies			
Formally stated	5	1	3
Ad-hoc basis	4	6	8
Functional Area Policies			
Marketing			
Formally stated	4	2	3
Ad-hoc basis	5	5	8
Product-Line			
Formally stated	5	2	3
Ad-hoc basis	4	5	8
Manpower			
Formally stated	4		3
Ad-hoc basis	5	7	8
Participation in Policy-Formulation			
Policy committee made of only top executives	5	1	3
Top executive only	4	6	8
Review of Policies			
Yearly	4		2
Six-monthly		1	
Monthly	1		
Ad-hoc – when needed	4	6	9

advanced the following positions which suggest a positive relationship between participation in policy formulation and implementation of these policies:

1. Groups are superior to individuals as sources of policy.
2. When those affected by a policy know the reason for it and can participate in its formulation, they are more likely to accept it.

Behavior (Glenview, Ill.: Scott, Foresman & Co., 1969), pp. 171-187. Similar propositions are tested more rigorously by Tannenbaum and his colleagues. See A. S. Tannenbaum (editor), *Control in Organizations* (New York: McGraw-Hill Book Company, 1969).

TABLE 3-2. *Policy Areas of Concern (Questionnaire Survey)*

Areas of Concern	U.S. Subsidiary (n = 23)	Local Firm (n = 76)
Pricing	17 (73.9)*	39 (51.3)
Personnel selection	18 (78.3)	55 (72.4)
Plant investment	16 (69.6)	49 (64.5)
Salary and wages	17 (73.19)	34 (44.7)
Control	15 (65.2)	40 (52.6)
Technology	14 (60.9)	35 (46.1)
Borrowing	12 (52.2)	40 (52.6)
Product-line	13 (56.5)	44 (57.9)
Purchasing	12 (52.2)	23 (30.3)
Acquisitions and expansion	10 (43.5)	23 (30.3)
Advertising budget	9 (39.1)	13 (17.1)
Training	9 (39.1)	27 (35.5)
Employee relations	9 (39.1)	15 (19.7)

* Figures in parentheses represent the percentage of the total number of companies in each category (U.S. vs. Local). Percentages do not add up to 100% because many companies mentioned more than one factor.

3. Policy creates a perceived freedom of action on the part of group participants because they are better able to predict the actions of others and know how they themselves are expected to behave.

The authors have supported these propositions with empirical data. Of course, these empirical studies were undertaken in the American context and one has no way of knowing their relevance for the Chinese society. However, in our questionnaire survey more than two-thirds of the Chinese executives (n = 73) agreed that the group goal-setting is better than the individual goal-setting.

Whatever the advantage of goal-setting by a group may be, we found very little evidence that the companies in Taiwan follow this practice. As data in Table 3-1 indicates, in most of the companies only top executives or the owner himself formulates major policies. In many companies even the senior and next to the senior-level executives are only vaguely aware of their firm's policies.

A well-qualified Chinese executive (M.B.A. from a major U.S. university) working for a U.S. subsidiary seems to have summed up the general situation in Taiwan. "All executives are playing games to get the favor of General Manager .... All policy-decisions are made by the big boss, and we are counted as nothing. ... All rules and regulations are given to us ... we do meet in committees, but everybody is just playing games to get favor of General Manager."

The review procedure is also haphazard. Fewer than one-third of the companies interviewed have established review procedures.

A lack of participation in policy-formulation and ad-hoc review procedure is also reflected among the companies surveyed by questionnaire. A large majority of the responding companies (n = 71) indicate that their policies are made by the chief executive or the owner himself, and they verbally communicate these policies to senior and middle-level executives.

To sum up, policy guidelines as a controlling device are underutilized in the Taiwan companies. Only the American subsidiaries are somewhat articulate in utilizing policy statements as control measures.

OTHER CONTROL TECHNIQUES USED IN THE COMPANIES IN TAIWAN

As mentioned earlier, attempts were made to solicit information concerning the use of the following control techniques in companies in Taiwan: (a) standard settings for production of goods and services, blue-collar workers, clerical employees, and supervisory personnel, (b) cost and budgetary controls, (c) statistical quality controls, (d) time and motion study, (e) equipment maintenance, (f) return on investment, and (g) profit and loss statement.

Standard Settings

The setting of standards is prerequisite to any control measure. Unless the standards are set, measurement of performance becomes less meaningful.

Data presented in Table 3-3 shows that the American and Japanese subsidiaries are more concerned with the production standards. A majority of these companies establish formal standards for production and blue-collar workers. Among the local firms, less than one-third of the companies undertake formal standard settings. There are only a few companies which show concern for clerical and supervisory personnel. This lack of interest in salaried employees is reflected by a Japanese executive in these words: "What is more important for us is production ... we closely watch what is happening on the assembly line ... for other employees ... we do not worry ... they do not produce anything."

TABLE 3-3. *Standard Settings in the American and Japanese Subsidiaries and Local Firms in Taiwan*

Firm	Production of Goods and Services	Blue-Collar Workers	Clerical Employees	Supervisory Personnel
U.S. Subsidiaries (*n* = *9*)				
Formally and systematically done	7	5	3	3
Ad-hoc basis	2	4	6	6
Japanese Subsidiaries (*n* = *7*)				
Formally and systematically done	6	4	1	1
Ad-hoc basis	1	3	6	6
Local Firms (*n* = *11*)				
Formally and systematically done	3	3	3	3
Ad-hoc basis	8	8	8	8

Standard settings are mostly done by top executives or owners themselves.

Cost and Budgetary Controls

Both the American and Japanese subsidiaries pay considerable attention to cost and budgetary controls. More than two-thirds of these companies establish cost and budgetary controls. Among the local firms, less than one-half do the same. There are considerable differences, however, among the type of personnel undertaking cost and budgetary controls. American subsidiaries utilize qualified and trained personnel to undertake these tasks, while in the Japanese and local companies, either the top executives themselves (whether qualified or not) or some other unqualified personnel are in charge of these functions.

Other Control Techniques

Many of the companies in Taiwan are less concerned about such control measures as time and motion study, periodical management

TABLE 3-4. *Scope and Types of Controls in American and Japanese Subsidiaries and Local Firms*

Scope and Type of Controls	U.S. Subsidiary (n = 9)	Japanese Subsidiary (n = 7)	Local Firm (n = 11)
1. Cost Control			
Done for all products	8	2	3
Done for major products	1	4	1
Done at random			3
Not done at all		1	4
2. Personnel Responsible for Cost-Control			
Qualified personnel in separate departments	9	1	3
Qualified personnel in respective departments			
Unqualified personnel		6	4
Not done at all			4
3. Budgeting and Resource Allocation			
Done for entire firm	7	4	5
Done for each plant or department	1	1	
Not done – Ad-hoc basis	1	2	6
4. Personnel Responsible for Budgeting and Resource Allocation			
Top management/owner		5	
Controller-separate department	8		3
Divisional managers	1		2
Not done – Ad-hoc basis		2	6
5. Time and Motion Study			
Formally done	3	2	
Not done	6	5	11
6. Equipment Maintenance			
Done systematically by qualified and trained personnel	8	6	5
Done on Ad-hoc basis by unskilled personnel	1	1	6

TABLE 3-4 (*continued*)

Scope and Type of Controls	U.S. Subsidiary (n = 9)	Japanese Subsidiary (n = 7)	Local Firm (n = 11)
7. Statistical Quality Control			
Done for all products	5	5	3
Done for major products	3	2	
Randomly done	1		8
8. Personnel Responsible for Quality Control			
Qualified personnel	8	6	3
Unqualified personnel	1	1	8

audit system, return on investment, and profit and loss statements. As can be seen from Table 3-4, only three of the nine U.S. subsidiaries, and two of the seven Japanese subsidiaries utilize time and motion study as controlling devices. The proportion of those using the management audit system, return on investment, and profit and loss statement is quite minimal.

A majority of companies, however, pay considerable attention to equipment maintenance. Among these, American and Japanese subsidiaries outnumber the local ones. High equipment cost, particularly on imported machinery, may explain the greater concern in this area.

Similarly, a statistical quality control technique is popular among American and Japanese subsidiaries and a few of the local firms. Many of these firms employ well-qualified personnel to undertake statistical quality control.

INTERNATIONAL COMPARISON

Controlling practices of companies studied (n = 92) in Argentina, Brazil, India, the Philippines, and Uruguay are as follows.[5]

Major Policies

A majority of the American subsidiaries in these five developing countries have formal policy statements on important aspects of their

[5] Anant R. Negandhi and S. B. Prasad, *Comparative Management* (New York: Appleton-Century-Crofts, 1971), pp. 81-90.

enterprises and make serious attempts to utilize the guidelines provided in major policies as control measures. In the case of local firms, however, only one-half of the companies studied in India and the Philippines seem to have formulated and documented their major policies.

Functional policies in the areas of product-mix and marketing are formulated by a somewhat greater number of local firms in these countries.

There is a clear indication toward centralization in decision-making with respect to major-policy-making. For example, data from companies in India indicates that in more than half of the companies studied (n = 34), the chief executive alone makes such policies. Such a situation exists in 13 of the 17 Indian-owned firms and in 6 of the 17 U.S. subsidiaries. A committe form of decision-making is practiced in the other half of these companies. Data from the Philippines shows a more or less similar trend.

In Argentina, Brazil, and Uruguay, however, only the chief executive formulates the company's major policies. With respect to functional policies, some form of group-decision-making is apparent in the majority of the companies studied.

The local firms in Taiwan are closer to the firms in Latin American countries in terms of documentation and participation in major policy-making. That is, policies are made on a contingency basis, and the chief executive or owner himself is responsible for policy-decisions. The same is true about the Japanese subsidiaries in Taiwan. American subsidiaries in Taiwan, however, are not much different from American subsidiaries in the other five developing countries.

Other Control Measures

Standard settings for production employees and middle-management personnel, as well as quality control procedures, are utilized by a majority of the companies studied in the five developing countries. Financial controls in terms of management audit, return on investment, cost and budgetary control are not utilized by many companies, particularly not by local firms.

There are also considerable differences among the U.S. subsidiaries and local firms regarding their methods of administrating various control devices. For example, in the U.S. subsidiaries, standards for both production employees and middle-management personnel are set by committees while in the local firms, mainly the chief executives or owners undertake these tasks. Also, the quality control is undertaken by qualified and trained personnel in the U.S. subsidiaries whereas, in many local firms, this task is performed by less qualified and trained personnel. However, there is no dearth of qualified and trained personnel in these countries.

Environmental Factors and Control Measures

Our interviews with the managers in these six developing countries failed to disclose any serious environmental constraints in utilizing modern control techniques, although, as we saw above, many of the local firms are not utilizing such control measures.

The reasons given by the executives for their lack of concern for necessary control measures are mainly in terms of seller's market conditions and insufficient "managerial know-how" concerning control methods. Of course, the seller's market rationale was advanced by the executives in Argentina, Brazil, India, the Philippines, and Uruguay. While the Chinese executives are more concerned about excessive price competition, none of the executives in any of these six countries is able to provide convincing arguments in terms of socio-cultural constraints for instituting control devices.

Contrary to the prevailing belief, our inquiry also failed to disclose any serious non-availability of qualified and trained native personnel to perform control tasks. Quite the reverse, we found higher unemployment rates among educated and qualified persons in those countries.

This evidence, as well as our interviews with the executives in American subsidiaries and progressive local firms which were able to institute comprehensive control measures, seem to indicate that controlling is a function of the managerial policy. In other words, if the firm wishes to employ certain control measures, it may successfully be able to do so without undue environmental constraints.

As stated in the beginning of this chapter, the control function is closely related to both planning and organization structure. In the preceding chapter we analyzed the planning practices of companies in Taiwan. In the next chapter we will examine the various aspects of organizing.

CHAPTER IV

ORGANIZATION

Introduction

The management literature contains a variety of definitions on the concept of organization. It has been viewed as: (a) a system of communication; (b) a means of facilitating decision-making; (c) a social system involving interpersonal relationships; and (d) a managerial function of organizing which involves grouping activities, establishing authority-responsibility relationships, coordinating different functional activities in pursuit of achieving overall organizational objectives and goals, and delegation of authority.[1] Among all these issues, two subjects have received concerted attention from management scholars and practicing managers: delegation of authority and decentralization in decision-making.

Particularly in the last two decades or so, management concepts such as "participative management," "theory Y," and "management by objectives" have become catch-all expressions among theorists and practitioners. In essence, all of these concepts convey the message to delegate authority and push decision-making power to the lower levels.

Purpose of this Chapter

In this study we view organization as a managerial function of organizing. Accordingly, data for the following topics were collected from the companies studied:

1. Grouping of activities
2. Layers of hierarchy
3. Authority definition and uses of organization charts

[1] Earnest Dale, *Organization* (New York: American Management Association, 1967), p. 1.

4. Delegation of authority and decentralization in decision-making
5. Uses of committees and conferences
6. Decision-making regarding major and functional area policies
7. Executive views on decentralization

Before presenting the analysis of data collected in Taiwan, we shall briefly review the organizational practices observed in the American parent companies located in the U.S.

ORGANIZATIONAL PRACTICES IN THE UNITED STATES

Findings Concerning 15 Parent Companies

Data collected from the 15 U.S. parent companies indicate the majority of these companies are organized on the basis of functions – i.e., production, sales, accounting, finance, etc. Organization through product-line is evident only in a few of these companies, but the executives interviewed indicated a trend in this direction.

The U.S. parent companies studied were all large-scale firms employing from 500 to 180,000 persons; therefore, data on the layers of hierarchy are not strictly comparable. The highest number of layers in the organization structure of these companies is 11; the average number of layers is 7.

Thirteen out of 15 companies revise and update organization charts on a regular basis (every three to five years). A majority of the compnies does more than pay lip-service to the delegation of authority. Decision-making, in many instances, is a group process. In all the companies, there are service and staff departments.

Findings of Other Reseachers

Holden, Pederson and Germane,[2] who studied large-scale companies in the U.S. during 1941 and 1968, found the following trends in their organization set-ups:

a. Relative stability of organization structure.
b. Changing attitudes toward committees; fewer standing committees and more ad-hoc task forces.
c. Grouping of activities on the basis of product and geographical divisions versus functional aspects of business.

[2] P. E. Holden, C. A. Pederson, and G. E. Germane, *Top Management* (New York: McGraw-Hill Book Company, 1968), pp. 5-6.

d. Emergence of product and program managers as new elites.
e. An increased number of vice-presidents with a consequent decrease in span of control for the chief executives.
f. No change in the role and function of Boards of Directors; the board member is merely vested with the trusteeship function.
g. The trend toward adherence to the decentralization philosophy, although changes in environmental factors, growth, complexity, and greater interdependence of divisions resulted in greater centralized controls for such activities as setting corporate objectives, strategic planning, determination of basic policies, finance, accounting systems, basic research, bargaining with unions, and public relations work.

Similar trends also were found by Dale[3] in his surveys of 100 large and 41 medium-size U.S. firms undertaken in 1952 and 1966.

Empirical investigations have been generated to pinpoint specific advantages and disadvantages of work-division specialization, departmentalization, and delegation of authority. On the basis of various empirical studies, Filley and House[4] recently formulated the following propositions or hypotheses concerning these factors:

a. Division of labor leads to decreased job satisfaction, but increased productivity.
b. Departmentalization by product or customer will result in less attention to professional or functional skill and more attention to client needs than departmentalization by function or process.
c. A clear definition of roles is requisite for effective delegation of responsibility and authority and acceptance of accountability.
d. Responsibility and authority for decision and task accomplishment should be delegated to the lowest level in the organization at which there is sufficient competence and information for effective decision-making or task performance.
e. Organizations with a clear and single flow of authority (unity of command) are more satisfying to their members and realize more effective economic performance and goal achievement than do organizations without a single clear flow of authority.

[3] Dale, *op. cit.*

[4] Alan C. Filley and Robert J. House, *Management Process and Organizational Behavior* (Glenview, Illinois: Scott, Foresman and Company, 1969), pp. 221-254, 301-308, 311-314.

f. Role conflict is associated with decreased satisfaction and decreased organizational effectiveness.

ORGANIZATIONAL PRACTICES OF INDUSTRIAL FIRMS IN TAIWAN

Grouping of Activities: Departmentation

All three types of companies in Taiwan – American subsidiaries, Japanese subsidiaries, and local companies – are organized on the basis of traditional business functions. In contrast to recent trends in the United States, none of the companies studied group activities on the basis of products, geographical divisions, customers, or projects. This, of course, reflects both a lack of sophistication in Taiwan's present economic environment and a smaller size of companies.

There are, however, considerable differences among these three types of companies concerning their relative organizations and the emphasis placed on different units. As can be seen from Table 4-1, a

TABLE 4-1. *Organization of Specific Departments*

Department	U.S. Subsidiary (n = 9)	Japanese Subsidiary (n = 7)	Local Firm (n = 11)
How are the Budgeting and Cost Accounting Departments Organized?			
Well-organized qualified personnel	8	1	3
Not well-organized – randomly done	1	6	8
How is the Personnel Department Organized?			
Separately organized – qualified personnel	3	0	1
Separately organized – semi-qualified personnel	1	0	1
Not separately organized – plant manager, general manager, and owner in charge	5	7	9

TABLE 4-1 (*continued*)

Department	U.S. Subsidiary (n = 9)	Japanese Subsidiary (n = 7)	Local Firm (n = 11)
How is the Purchasing Department Organized?			
Well organized with qualified personnel	3	0	2
Not well organized (or randomly organized) without qualified personnel	6	7	9
How is the Sales Department Organized?			
Well organized with qualified personnel	4	0	2
Not well organized (or randomly organized) without qualified personnel	5	7	9
How is the Production Department Organized?			
Great specialization – divisional work	8	3	7
Organized loosely – without much concern for specialization or division of work	1	4	4

greater number of the American subsidiaries have well organized budgeting and cost control, personnel, sales, purchasing, and production functions. The Japanese subsidiaries and local companies are well organized in the production area, but they put much less emphasis on other functions. It is interesting to note that, of all these functions, their personnel function receives the most cursory treatment in Taiwan.

Number of Departments

There are no differences in the number of departments or divisions among these three types of companies. They all seem to have between five and seven departments. The questionnaire survey undertaken with the larger sample (n = 99) also indicates the same pattern. Here, for example, we find that 72 per cent of the U.S. subsidiaries and 66 per cent of the local firms have five or less departments in their organizations. However, the related question of "How many departments have separate managers," reveals that the American subsidiaries have distinct departments with departmental heads or managers while, in the local firms, many managers control more than one department. In other words, the concept of departmentation is much clearer in the American subsidiaries than in the local firms.

STAFF AND SERVICE DEPARTMENTS

The degree of organizational sophistication can also be seen through the existence of service and staff departments. During the last two decades or so, there has been a growing trend in the U.S. industries to utilize specialized and expert knowledge through staff and service departments. In many of the U.S. companies such personnel play an important and pivotal role in policy-making and the company's long range plans and strategies.[5]

Examination of data collected from the companies in Taiwan, however, shows relatively less use of such specialized staff personnel.

As can be seen in Table 4-2, a little less than half of the American subsidiaries have staff positions. Among the Japanese subsidiaries and local companies, the use of such staff personnel is rare. Only 1 out of 7 Japanese companies and 2 out of 11 local firms have one staff position in their organizations. The latter companies, however, do not seem to use their staff personnel as extensively as their American subsidiary counterparts.

Service departments are more popular among all three types of the companies. Among these, however, American and Japanese subsidiaries utilize service departments more extensively.

DELEGATION OF AUTHORITY AND DECENTRALIZATION

As mentioned earlier, the concepts of decentralization and delegation of authority have received considerable attention from management scholars, as well as practicing managers. In many U.S. companies, decentralization is not only a managerial practice, but it also constitutes a firm's philosophy and orientation. This has been ex-

[5] See Holden *et al.*, *op. cit.*

TABLE 4-2. *Staff Positions and Service Departments*

	U.S. Subsidiary (n = 9)	Japanese Subsidiary (n = 7)	Local Firm (n = 11)
Are there any staff positions?			
Yes	4	1	2
No	5	6	9
How many staff positions are there?			
1			
2	2	1	2
3	2	0	0
None	5	6	9
What is their (staff) authority?			
Recommending			
Gather data	2	1	0
Set policy			
Comb. 1 & 2	1	0	2
Comb. 1 & 2 & 3	1	0	0
None	5	6	9
Are there any "Service Departments"?			
Yes	9	6	5
No	0	1	6
To whom do they report?			
General management	4	4	4
Department heads	5	2	1
N. A./not applicable	0	1	6

plained by Koontz and O'Donnell in these words:

> Although closely related to delegation, decentralization is more; it is a philosophy of organization and management, implying both selective dispersal and concentration of authority. It requires far more than simple handing authority to subordinates. ... Indeed, decentralization encompasses all areas of management.[6]

[6] H. Koontz and C. O'Donnell, *Principles of Management* (4th edition; New York: McGraw-Hill Book Company, 1968), p. 350.

Empirically, decentralization has been linked to higher management effectiveness, employee satisfaction, morale, and productivity.[7] Recent research findings, however, seem to indicate some reservations about a positive relationship between decentralization and management effectiveness, and employee satisfaction.

Researchers such as Woodward[8], and Lawrence and Lorsch,[9] for example, have found that decentralization in decision-making is more effective under unstable environmental conditions while centralization may be more appropriate under stable environmental conditions.

In the same vein, some cross-cultural management scholars have argued that the decentralization concept is not applicable in developing countries.[10]

Without getting involved in a normative judgment about the utility of the decentralization concept among industrial firms in Taiwan, our aim was simply to measure the degree of decentralization in these companies and to establish the relationship between decentralization and management effectiveness.

Measure of Decentralization

Various criteria or factors have been suggested to measure the degree of decentralization in decision-making in a given organization. For example, the Aston Research Group[11] has included the following factors to measure organizational structure arrangements:

1. Overall role specialization
2. Functional specialization
3. Overall standardization of procedures

[7] Rensis Likert, *The Human Organization: Its Management and Value* (New York: McGraw-Hill Book Company, Inc., 1967).

[8] Joan Woodward, *Industrial Organization: Theory and Practice* (London: Oxford University Press, 1965). See also a report on her recent research in: "Technology, Managerial Control, and Organizational Behavior," in A. R. Negandhi *et al.* (eds.) *Organizational Behavior Models* (Kent, Ohio: Bureau of Economic and Business Research, Kent State University, 1970), Chapter 2.

[9] Paul R. Lawrence and Jay W. Lorsch, *Organization and Environment* (Homewood, Ill.: Richard D. Irwin, Inc., 1969).

[10] Richard F. Gonzalez and Claude McMillan, Jr., "The Universality of American Management Philosophy," *Journal of the Academy of Management*, IV, No. 1 (April, 1961), pp. 33-41.

[11] D. Hickson, D. S. Pugh, and D. C. Pheysey, "Operations Technology and Organization Structure: An Empirical Reappraisal," *Administrative Science Quarterly*, XIV, No. 3 (1969), pp. 378-397.

4. Overall formalization (documentation)
5. Overall centralization of decisions
6. Autonomy of the organization
7. Standardization of procedures for selection and advancement, etc.
8. Subordinate – superior ratio
9. Formalization of role performance recording
10. Percentage of work-flow superordinates

Evan[12] has suggested six indices to evaluate the hierarchy of authority in organizations. These are:

1. Span of control
2. The number of levels of authority, from top management to worker
3. Ratio of administrative personnel to production workers
4. "Time-span of discretion" ("the maximum length of time the employee is authorized to make decisions on his own initiative which commit a given amount of the resources of the organization")
5. The degree of centralization in decision-making
6. The degree of limitation on the right of management to make decisions

In order to measure the degree of decentralization in decision-making among American and Japanese subsidiaries and local firms in Taiwan, we collected data on some nine items. These include layers of hierarchy, locus of decision-making regarding major policies and functional areas (production, marketing, manpower, etc.), policy and standard setting, and information-sharing. The list of factors investigated are given in Table 8-5 (Chapter 8).

Information on the following items gave us a good insight into the actual decision-making processes that exist in the companies studied.[13]

1. Layers of hierarchy
2. Authority definition
3. Organization chart
4. Authority overlap
5. Use of committees and conferences

[12] William M. Evan, "Indices of the Hierarchical Structure of Industrial Organizations," *Management Science*, IX (April, 1963), pp. 470-473.

[13] Similar information was collected from companies in other developing countries. For findings see A. R. Negandhi and S. B. Prasad, Comparative Management (New York: Appleton-Century-Crofts) 1971.

6. Decision-making regarding major policies and functional areas

We shall first analyze data concerning the above factors in a little more detail, then discuss the decentralization indices for three sets of companies.

Layers of Hierarchy

As shown in Table 4-3, organizational hierarchies are higher in both Japanese subsidiaries and local firms in Taiwan; their American counterparts have few organizational layers. Specifically, 6 out of 9 U.S. subsidiaries have 5 to 7 organizational layers, while only 2 of the 7 Japanese subsidiaries and 3 of the 11 local companies belong to this category.

Organization Chart and Authority Definition

Data on the existence of organization charts indicate that the charts are popular among many companies. However, the actual use of such organizational charts is minimal in the Japanese and local companies. This can be seen when we examine the data on authority definition. In answer to the question, "How do you know what your authority is?" management personnel in 5 of the 7 Japanese subsidiaries and 6 of the 11 local firms indicated that they know their authority through verbal conversations with their superiors. Such a situation exists in only 3 of the 9 U.S. subsidiaries.

An inquiry into the overlap of authority also suggests that the authority of managerial personnel is diffuse rather than specific in a greater number of Japanese subsidiaries and local firms. These firms also maintain considerable secrecy in both documenting and communicating authority lines and organizational charts. This type of secrecy was highlighted during our interview with the president of one local company. When asked about the nature of an organization chart he stood up, locked the office door, opened his safe, and pulled out the organization chart. He said "this is special treat . . . I have not shown this chart to anybody, not even my vice-president . . . this is my secret." Although such an extreme situation was not found in other Japanese and local companies, it is nevertheless considered a privilege among management personnel to have seen the organizational charts of their firms.

To a great extent, such organizational practices, although they appear strange to American students of management, reflect collective orientations prevailing in the oriental society. Yoshino's[14] penetrating analysis of the management scene in Japan exemplified the type of situation we found among the Japanese and local companies in Taiwan. In his study Yoshino reports that:

> One of the distinct features of the Japanese corporate organization is that it is structured in collective organizational units rather than in terms of individual positions. This is very evident in the organization chart in which the corporate organization is depicted in terms of divisions, departments and sections, rather than the individual positions; ... Japanese managers are much less concerned about who performs a task and where the responsibility lies than about how individuals within organizations work together harmoniously toward the accomplishment of the goals of the collectivity.[15]

Uses of Committees and Conferences

Committees and conferences can be utilized for both decision-making and providing necessary information to company personnel. In both instances it represents the management's willingness to share decision-making powers with subordinates. Data shown in Table 4-3, indicate all three types of companies are eager to utilize those mechanisms.

However, our inquiry into the working of committees revealed that, in many of the local firms and Japanese subsidiaries, committees are used to issue "orders" to various functional managers. Even among the American subsidiaries, committees are used to sound off decisions which were made either at the U.S. headquarters or by the chief executive in Taiwan. In other words, committees are not used extensively for decision-making.

This can easily be seen when we examine the data concerning major and functional area policies. For example, data reported in Table 4-4 show that, in the majority of local firms and Japanese subsidiaries, the chief executive or owner himself makes decisions regarding major policies, marketing, product line, and manpower. Among the U.S. subsidiaries, less than 50% of the firms indicate group decision-making in these areas.

[14] M. Y. Yoshino, *Japan's Managerial System* (Cambridge: M.I.T. Press, 1968).
[15] *Ibid.*, p. 202.

TABLE 4-3. *Organizational Characteristics*

Items/Questions	U.S. Subsidiary (n = 9)	Japanese Subsidiary (n = 7)	Local Firm (n = 11)
Layers of hierarchy			
15 and more	0	0	1
8 to 15	3	6	7
5 to 7	6	1	3
Existence of organization charts			
Yes	6	6	7
No	3	1	4
How do you know what your authority is?			
Verbal	3	5	6
Written, through org. charts	6	0	3
Learned on job	0	2	2
Does any other supervisor overlap your authority?			
Many	0	1	2
Some	2	3	3
None	7	3	6
Does any supervisor in one department, line, or staff, have any direct or indirect authority in other departments?			
Yes	3	3	5
No	5	3	4
Not clear	1	0	1
Not available	0	1	1
What use is made of committees in your organization?			
Much	3	0	2
Some	4	6	7
None	2	1	2
What use is made of conferences in the company (or in your department)?			
Much	1	0	1
Some	6	6	5
None	1	1	4
Not Available	1	0	1

TABLE 4-4. *Decision-Making for Major and Functional Policies*

Items	U.S. Subsidiary (n = 9)	Japanese Subsidiary (n = 7)	Local Firm (n = 11)
Major Policies (mergers, new plants, etc.)			
Who makes them?			
Owner/chief executive	4	6	7
Executive committee (with top level executives only)	5	1	3
General committee made of all levels of personnel			
Top and middle level executives	0	0	1
Who makes policies regarding marketing?			
Owner/chief executives only	4	4	7
Committee made of functional managers	3	2	3
Functional managers concerned			
Committee made of marketing department personnel			
Not clear-cut	2	1	1
Policy-making for product-line			
Chief executive only	3	5	9
Executive committee of functional managers	5	2	2
General executive committee	–	–	–
Functional manager	–	–	–
Functional managers' committee	–	–	–
Not Available	1	0	0
Compensation and promotion aspects			
Policies for selection and promotion of executive personnel made by:			
Chief executive/owner	5	6	10
Top executive committee	4	1	1

TABLE 4-4 (*continued*)

Items	U.S. Subsidiary (n = 9)	Japanese Subsidiary (n = 7)	Local Firm (n = 11)
Selection and promotion of clerical workers			
Chief executive/owner	2	4	7
Top executive committee	1	3	1
General committee	3	0	0
Functional manager	3	0	3
Supervisor			
Dept. committee			
Ad hoc			
Selection and promotion of blue-collar employees			
Chief executive/owner	0	2	4
Top executive committee			
General committee	1	1	1
Functional manager	6	4	3
Supervisor	1	0	3
Dept. committee	1	0	0
Ad hoc			

Decentralization Index

As mentioned earlier, for examining the overall degree of decentralization in decision-making, we compiled and collected information on nine items. These cover a broad range of activity from major policy-making to decisions regarding the setting of standards for blue-collar workers. In order to compute the overall decentralization index, we assigned numerical values of 1 to 3, depending upon the level of decision-making. (The greater the consultation in decision-making, the lower the numerical value; e.g., if the decisions are made through consultation with all levels of management personnel, the firm will be assigned one point; if decisions are made by the chief executive or owner himself, it will be assigned three points). The decentralization index was derived by dividing the total number of points made by each firm by the number of factors investigated (9). This gave us a minimum index of 1.0 ("highly decentralized") to a maximum of 3.0 ("highly centralized").

Decentralization Index for Three Types of Firms

The decentralization index for the U.S. subsidiaries varies from 1.61 to 2.91, the average being 2.16. The index for Japanese subsidiaries varies from 1.88 to 2.94. The average index for these firms is 2.42. The index for local companies varies from 1.85 to 2.94, the average being 2.40.

Examination of average indices for these three types of firms thus shows that the U.S. subsidiaries are relatively more decentralized than both Japanese and local companies in Taiwan. The Japanese and local companies are almost identical in terms of their decision-making.

The distribution of companies in various categories of the decentralization index, shown in Table 4-5, indicates somewhat more clearly the degree of decentralization utilized by the three types of firms. Here, for example, we find that two-thirds of the U.S. subsidiaries have their decentralization index between 1.6 and 2.0. Only one Japanese subsidiary and three local firms fall into this category. In contrast, we find a greater number of Japanese subsidiaries (3 out of 7) and local firms (5 out of 11) have a decentralization index between 2.6 and 3.0.

Data on the decentralization index thus supports our overall contention that American subsidiaries are relatively more decentralized than Japanese and local companies in Taiwan. It also indicates that there are no appreciable differences between Japanese subsidiaries and local firms.

International Comparisons

Data collected on identical items from American subsidiaries and

TABLE 4-5. *Decentralization Indices for the U.S. and Japanese Subsidiaries and Local Firms in Taiwan*

Decentralization Index	U.S. Subsidiary (n = 9)	Japanese Subsidiary (n = 7)	Local Firm (n = 11)
1.0 to 1.5			
1.6 to 2.0	6	1	3
2.1 to 2.5	1	4	3
2.6 to 3.0	2	3	5
Average Index	2.16	2.42	2.40

TABLE 4-6. *Decentralization Index for the U.S. Subsidiaries and Local Firms in India**

Decentralization Index	U.S. Subsidiary (n = 15)	Local Indian Company (n = 15)
1.0 to 1.5	5	2
1.6 to 2.0	6	7
2.1 to 2.5	3	3
2.6 to 3.0	1	3
Average Index	1.77	2.06

* Reproduced from Anant R. Negandhi, "American Management Abroad: A Comparative Study of Management Practices of American Subsidiaries and Local Firms in Developing Countries," *Management International Review*, 1971, No. 4/5, p. 101. Permission of the journal is greatfully acknowledged.

local firms in Argentina, Brazil, India, the Philippines, and Uruguay suggest the following comparative profile.[16]

1. American subsidiaries in Taiwan are relatively more centralized than those in India and the Philippines. There are no appreciable differences among the American subsidiaries in Argentina, Brazil, Uruguay, and Taiwan.
2. The local companies in India are relatively more decentralized than those in Taiwan. This can be seen from the data prasented in Table 4-6.
3. The American subsidiaries are relatively more decentralized as compared to counterpart local firms in all the six countries.[17]

Decentralization and Management Effectiveness

In the beginning of this chapter we pointed out the conflicting findings concerning the relationship between decentralization and management effectiveness. Briefly, it was stated that some researchers have found positive relationships between these two variables while others have argued for the conditional relationships. That is, decentralization may be more effective under unstable environmental working conditions while centralization may be more effective under stable conditions.

[16] For more details see Negandhi-Prasad, *op. cit.*, Chapter 4, pp. 51-66.

[17] Similar conclusions are drawn by Papageorge in his study in Greece. See A. J. Papageorge, *Transferability of Management: The Case Study of the U.S. and Greece* (Unpublished Ph.D. thesis, University of California, Los Angeles, 1967).

It was also pointed out that cross-cultural management researchers have added another dimension. They have, in brief, argued that decentralization may be less suitable for developing countries.

In order to explore the relationship between decentralization and management effectiveness, we computed Spearman's Rank correlation. The correlation coefficient between these two variables is 0.66. These data are given in Table 8-4 (Chapter 8). We shall discuss more about the relationships among various indices in Chapter 8.

Culture and Decentralization

Are there any inherent cultural differences between the American and Chinese executives which may account for the differing degree of decentralization in their respective organizations? Many management studies undertaken in cross-cultural settings seem to emphasize the cultural differences among various countries. A brief review of pertinent cross-cultural findings seems to pinpoint the following differences among managers in different countries.[18]

1. U.S. managers are equally concerned with people and production while Japanese and South American managers are more concerned with production than with people (Mouton and Bakke).[19]
2. The employees in Brazil preferred a participative-democratic style of leadership, while in Japan employees preferred more authoritarian leaders. Over all, IBM employees in some 45 countries preferred consultative-type leadership (IBM Survey, Sirota).[20]
3. In terms of managerial attitudes and behavior, there seems to be a cultural cluster plus a cluster of developing countries which are not related in terms of culture as much as those of economic growth (Haire, Ghiselli, and Porter).[21]

[18] For more details see G. V. Barrett and B. M. Bass, "Comparative Surveys of Managerial Attitudes and Behavior," in *Comparative Management: Teaching, Research and Training*, ed. by J. Boddewyn (New York: Graduate School of Business Administration, 1970), pp. 179-207.

[19] J. Mouton and R. Blake, "Issues in Transnational Organization Development," in *Managing for Accomplishment*, ed. by B. M. Bass, R. C. Cooper, and J. A. Haas (Lexington, Mass.: Heath Lexington, 1970), pp. 208-224.

[20] D. Sirota, "International Survey of Job Goals and Beliefs" (paper presented at 16th International Congress of Applied Psychology, Amsterdam, Netherlands, 1968).

[21] M. Haire, D. E. Ghiselli, and L. W. Porter, *Managerial Thinking: An International Study* (New York: John Wiley, 1966).

4. American managers have a more favorable attitude toward the average person's capacity for leadership and initiative than the British or Australians (Clark and McCabe).[22]
5. British managers are more attuned to an authoritarian style of leadership than American managers (Maier and Hoffman).[23]
6. Role-playing subordinates (in twelve countries) preferred more democratic relationships between supervisor and subordinates than the supervisors themselves (Thiagarajan and Deep).[24]
7. The more total influence everyone has in the system, the greater the total system efficiency (Tannenbaum, Rus).[25]
8. The Japanese managers shared information more than the Dutch military officers and Dutch managers; but Japanese managers have more difficulty in reaching a final decision (Hesseling and Konnen).[26]
9. There are definite cultural differences in supervisory preferences and style. India has been found authoritarian as compared with other countries (Meade and Whittaker).[27] Morale and productivity were higher under authoritarian than under democratic leadership in India; the results in the United States show the opposite effects (Meade).[28]
10. There seems to be a significant difference between managers from various countries, both in their problem-solving decisions and their listing of corporate objectives. Tentative data indicate that economic factors seem to be of more importance than cultural variables in this regard. For example, Indian and Columbian

[22] A. W. Clark and S. McCabe, "Leadership Beliefs of Australian Managers," *Journal of Applied Psychology*, LIV (1970), pp. 1-6.

[23] N. R. F. Maier and L. R. Hoffman, "Group Decision in England and the United States," *Personnel Psychology*, XV (1962), pp. 75-87.

[24] K. M. Thiagarajan and S. D. Deep, *A Cross-Cultural Study of Preferences for Participative Decision-making by Supervisors and Subordinates*, Technical Report 33, NONR 624 (14) (Rochester, New York: University of Rochester, Management Research Center, 1969).

[25] A. Tannenbaum, *Control in Organizations* (New York: McGraw-Hill, 1968). Also see V. Rus, "Influence Structure in Yugoslav Enterprise," *Industrial Relations*, IX (1970), pp. 148-160.

[26] P. Hesseling and E. E. Konnen, "Culture and Subculture in a Decision-making Exercise," *Human Relations*, XX (1969), pp. 31-51.

[27] R. D. Meade and J. D. Whittaker, "A Cross-Cultural Study of Authoritarianism," *Journal of Social Psychology*, LXXII (1967), pp. 3-7.

[28] R. D. Meade, "An Experimental Study of Leadership in India," *Journal of Social Psychology*, LXXII (1967), pp. 35-43.

managers put less emphasis on meeting competition, while their counterparts in developing countries are satisfied with the usual maintenance of their operations (Hoekstra, and Barrett, and Ryterband).[29]

11. Although there are similarities in manager orientation, G. W. England has advanced the thesis that cultural factors do make a difference in manager orientations (England, 1970).[30]
12. More democratic supervisory style is associated with greater growth in GNP and per capita income (Barrett and Franke).[31]

The overall findings seem to suggest the following:

1. There is no one way of doing things. Managers may achieve given objectives by various methods.
2. There is no universal applicability of either authoritarian or participating-democratic management styles. In general, the United States can best be characterized as having democratic-participative management style, while Germany, France, and most of the developing countries are authoritarian in their management styles. Authoritarian style is not necessarily dysfunctional in developing countries. This, perhaps, may be the "right" type of leadership.
3. More objective measures are brought to bear in making managerial decisions with respect to compensation, objectives, goal-settings, etc., in the developed countries, while many subjective judgments (emotions, religious beliefs) enter into the decision-making processes in developing countries.
4. There are enough similarities and differences among managers around the world. Similarities are explained in terms of industrialization or industrial sub-culture; differences are explained in

[29] M. H. R. Hoekstra, "Corporate Objectives: A Cross-Cultural Study of Simulated Managerial Behavior," in *Proceedings, XVIth International Congress of Applied Psychology* (Amsterdam: Swets & Zeitlinger, 1969), pp. 429-435. G. V. Barrett and E. C. Ryterband, "Cross-Cultural Comparisons of Corporate Objectives on Exercise Objectives" (paper presented at 76th Annual Convention, American Psychological Association, San Francisco, September ,1968).

[30] G. W. England, "Personal Value System Analysis as an Aid to Understanding Organizational Behavior: A Comparative study in Japan, Korea and the United States" (Presented at Exchange Seminar on Comparative Organizations, Amsterdam, Netherlands, March 23-27, 1970).

[31] G. V. Barrett and R. H. Franke, "Communication Preference and Performance: A Cross-Cultural Comparison," *Proceedings 77th Annual Convention*, American Psychological Association, 1969, pp. 597-598.

terms of cultural variables. Cultural factors are considered the most important influencing variables.

The Situation in Taiwan

To examine the American and Chinese executives' cultural orientations concerning decentralization, we asked them a series of semi-disguised questions by way of a questionnaire survey. Responses to this query failed to reveal significant differences between these two groups of executives in Taiwan. For example, American and Chinese executives share equally the feeling that the decision-making authority should be held tightly. However, the question concerning goal-setting (group vs. individual) reveals that both the American and Chinese executives prefer group-participation in goal-setting.

In terms of information-sharing, the American executives prefer a more open, freer flow of communication than the Chinese managers. The responses to these questions are summarized in Table 4-7.

Interview Responses

Executives of the American and Japanese subsidiaries and the local firms also were asked about the environmental and cultural factors impeding their decentralization plans. The following factors were most frequently mentioned by these executives:

1. Lack of training and education of the Chinese personnel
2. Respect for age
3. Extreme politeness and collectivity orientations of the oriental people
4. Extreme competition
5. Lack of financial resources

The first three factors, namely lack of training and education, respect for age, and the extreme politeness inherent in the Chinese cultural milieu are, in our opinion, real obstacles for those companies wishing to decentralize.

Summary

To recap, this chapter analyzed various aspects of the organizational set-up. These included: grouping of activities, layers of hierarchy, authority definition and uses of organization charts, delegation of authority and the degree of decentralization in decision-making, uses

TABLE 4-7. *Executives' Views on Decentralization (Questionnaire Survey)*

	AGREE		DISAGREE		UNDECIDED	
Questions	U.S. Sub.	Local Comp.	U.S. Sub.	Local Comp.	U.S. Sub.	Local
	%	%	%	%	%	%
1. Decision-making authority should be tightly held at the top level so that the company can "get on with the job."	61	63	30	22	9	15
2. Group goal-setting offers advantages that cannot be obtained by individual goal-setting.	70	76	13	11	17	13
3. A superior should give subordinates only that information which is necessary for them to do their immediate tasks.	22	56	78	36	–	8
4. A good leader should give detailed and complete instructions to the subordinates rather than giving them merely general directions and depending on their initiative to work out the details.	39	53	52	36	9	11
5. Management (and the Management Process) is essentially an "art" and can only be learned on the job, if the man is well-educated.	74	70	22	16	4	14

of committees and conferences, and executives' views on decentralization.

Our findings indicate that all three sets of companies in Taiwan are organized on a functional basis. There are no considerable differences among these firms in terms of number of departments in each company. It varies from five to seven departments. There is relatively less use of specialized staff personnel; only a few of the American subsidiaries seem to have staff positions. Service departments, however, are common in all three sets of companies.

Authority definition is clearer among U.S. subsidiaries, while there is considerable overlap of authority in Japanese subsidiaries and local firms. The organization chart is popular among all companies but its actual use is minimal.

American subsidiaries, relatively speaking, are more decentralized in their decision-making than both the Japanese subsidiaries and local companies in Taiwan.

At the end of this chapter we briefly reviewed the findings of other scholars concerning the impact of cultural and environmental factors on decentralization. Overall, these findings seem to indicate considerable impact of cultural factors on decentralization. However, our questionnaire survey failed to disclose any significant differences in the attitudes of American and Chinese executives in Taiwan.

Interviews with the company executives seem to reveal the impact of some cultural variable on decentralization. Our findings, however, failed to support the contention of many cross-cultural management researchers that decentralization is dysfunctional (less effective) in developing countries. On the contrary, we found a positive relationship between the degree of decentralization in decision-making and management effectiveness.

Decentralization per se is closely related to leadership style. In the next chapter we shall examine the leadership pattern and behavior found in Taiwan.

CHAPTER V

THE WORKER AND HIS BOSS: THE LEADERSHIP STYLES IN TAIWAN

Introduction

Both the concept and the function of leadership have been researched extensively, yet leadership is the least understood variable in the management discipline. A great deal of confusion exists on two major issues:

1. The impact of different styles of leadership on employee satisfaction, productivity, and management effectiveness;
2. The distinction between delegation of authority and the various types of leadership roles.

In this study we adopted the definition of leader provided by Warren Bennis, who says, "A leader is a person with power over others who exercises this power for the purpose of influencing their behavior." [1]

To evaluate the nature of leadership styles found in companies studied, we used the classification system developed by behavioral theorists of leadership.[2] These scholars have identified four types of leadership: autocratic, supportive (participative), instrumental, and the "greatman." As you will see below, we have made slight modifications in this classification system.

For our study, we distinguish the concepts of delegation of authority and leadership as follows: The degree of authority delegation spells out the scope of decision-making at each organizational level. A high degree of authority delegation suggests that a greater number of organizational decisions are made at the lower levels of management, while

[1] W. G. Bennis, "Leadership Theory and Administrative Behavior: The Problem of Authority," *Administrative Science Quarterly*, Vol. 4, December, 1959, pp. 259-301. Quoted from A. C. Filley and R. J. House, *Managerial Process and Organizational Behavior* (Glenview: Ill., Scott, Foresman and Company, 1968), p. 391.

[2] See for further details Filley and House, *op. cit.*, pp. 391-396.

a low degree of authority delegation suggests that a greater number of decisions are made at the higher levels.

In the management and organization theory literature, the concept of centralization and decentralization of authority is widely used to explain the degree of authority delegation in a given organization. We dealt with this aspect of organization in the last chapter.

In contrast to authority delegation, the concept of leadership conveys ways in which leaders motivate and influence the behavior of subordinates to achieve given goals or objectives. Generally speaking, the authoritarian leader makes all major decisions himself and issues orders to subordinates for their implementation. The consultative leader relies on his subordinates' consensus and encourages them to participate in the decision-making. The bureaucratic leader usually attempts to influence his subordinates by emphasizing the maze of rules, regulations, and procedures. The paternalistic leader, commonly found in developing countries, treats his subordinates as his "children" and adopts parental authority in decision-making.

Each type of leadership role is compatible with various degrees of authority delegation in a given organization. In other words, one can find an authoritarian leader in a decentralized organization, and a consultative leader in a centralized organization. However, many management scholars have equated decentralized organizations with consultative leaders, and centralized organizations with authoritarian leaders. This may not necessarily be the case in a given situation.[3]

Purpose of this Chapter

In this chapter we shall analyze data on the following factors:

1. Leadership styles used in the American and Japanese subsidiaries and local firms in Taiwan (n = 27).
2. Leaders' perception of subordinates in three sets of companies (n = 27).
3. Executives' view on leadership roles (questionnaire survey data, n = 99).
4. International comparisons of leadership styles.

[3] I am debted to my colleague, Professor Arlyn Melcher for this clarification. See his "Participation: A Critical Review of Research Findings" forthcoming in a book, *Organizational Behavior: Towards a System Approach*, Prentice-Hall.

Leadership Style in Companies in Taiwan

As stated earlier, the leadership-style classification system provided by behavioral theorists was slightly modified for this study. Based on intensive interviews with executives, middle, and lower level managers, and supervisory personnel in the companies studied, we attempted to categorize the leadership style used in each company in the following manner:

a. Consultative
b. Autocratic
c. Bureaucratic-autocratic
d. Paternalistic-autocratic

Companies utilizing a consultative type of leadership place a great deal of reliance on the opinion of subordinates, and a free discussion among superordinates and subordinates is most prevalent.

In companies characterized by authoritarian leadership style, the owner or chief executive generally makes all major and minor decisions.

Bureaucratic and paternalistic leaders are, in a sense, also authoritarian in their leadership roles; however, their attitudes are somewhat different. Bureaucratic leaders attempt to influence subordinates by emphasizing a maze of rules, regulations, and procedures outlined in a company manual; paternalistic leaders assume the "father figure" and have strong personal and emotional ties with their subordinates.

We attempted to evaluate leadership styles at three different levels: (a) top management, (b) middle management, (c) supervisory level.

Leadership at the Top Level

Data presented in Table 5-1 show the leadership styles used at different levels in companies in Taiwan. As can be seen from the table, Chinese top managerial personnel are largely paternalistic in their attitudes and behavior. In 7 out of the total 11 companies, this type of leadership is used at the top level. The American subsidiaries, in contrast, seem to prefer a consultative type of leadership and encourage employees to participate in decision-making. This leadership style predominates in 6 out of the 9 subsidiaries. The Japanese subsidiaries are more autocratic at the top level.

This top level leadership style in Japanese subsidiaries seems to be different from the one generally found in industrial organizations physically located in Japan. For example, Yoshino's recent study of

20 leading corporations in Japan suggests that, "the leader, in the Japanese context, is not a strong individual directing and inspiring the group to achieve objectives that he himself has set for the group. Rather, his main function is to create a proper atmosphere for the group's achieving its objectives. Thus, a commonly accepted approach in Japan is to assign only a limited range of functions to leadership and a rather passive role."[4]

Earlier studies by Abegglen,[5] Bennett and Ishino,[6] Harbison and Myers,[7] and Makane,[8] to name a few, suggest that the leader in Japan is more paternalistic than autocratic. As explained, the paternalistic leader has strong personal and emotional ties with his subordinates and, "he patronizes his followers who, in turn, submit to him."[9]

Paternalistic Outlook

It may be interesting to note that the concept of paternalistic management and leadership style conveys different meanings in different nations. Particularly in the Eastern societies, it underlies a basic religious-philosophical overtone. This is quite in contrast to the Western societies where paternalistic leadership and management simply suggest that a firm undertakes extensive social and welfare activities for its employees.

The religious-philosophical overtone embedded in the paternalistic management outlook in Japan, Taiwan, and other far Eastern countries is largely due to a Confucius' philosophy. Very briefly, Confucianism stresses benevolence, propriety, wisdom, and obedience, and these standards are applied within the specific, established social framework. This philosophy also "stresses five dyadic relationships and prescribes appropriate interaction for each: affection between father and son; respect and loyalty between master and servant;

[4] M. Y. Yoshino, *Japan's Managerial System* (Cambridge: M.I.T. Press, 1968), pp. 205-206.

[5] J. C. Abegglen, *The Japanese Factory: Aspects of its Social Organization* (Glencoe, Illinois: The Free Press, 1958).

[6] John W. Bennett and Iwao Ishino (eds.), *Paternalism in the Japanese Economy: Anthropological Studies of Oycibun-Kobun Patterns* (Minneapolis: University of Minnesota Press, 1963).

[7] F. Harbison and C. Myers, *Management in the Industrial World* (New York: McGraw-Hill Company, 1959).

[8] Chie Nakane, *Human Relations in a Vertically Related Society* (Tokyo: Kodansha, 1966). Quoted in Yoshino, *op. cit.*, p. 204.

[9] Yoshino, *op. cit.*, p. 209.

harmony between husband and wife; precedence between older and younger brothers; and trust between friends."[10]

The collectivity emphasized in Japanese organizations also is derived from Confucius' philosophy. As Yoshino states, under collectivism, "the primary function of a leader is to facilitate group performance, that is, to maximize the output of the entire group by avoiding friction within it and by developing a stronger sense of group identity and solidarity."[11]

Mr. Kitagawa, Chairman of Sumitomo Eletric Industries Limited, has clearly underscored the difference between Western and Eastern civilizations in this respect:

> Economic activities within Japanese society, in which an individual always behaves as a part of the whole society, differ from those in European and American societies, which are based on a philosophy of individualism under which rationalism is pursued from the standpoint of capital ... in a functional society where liberalism prevails and individuality is esteemed, specialization and preference for ability spread. On the contrary, in a society where groups dominate and people are dependent upon each other within a paternalistic structure, a system of lifetime employment is engendered, resulting in an emphasis on general harmony among persons and the denial of individuality.[12]

Our findings in Taiwan thus show the local Chinese companies pursue the paternalistic outlook as it exists in Japan, while Japanese subsidiaries in Taiwan seem to have restrained themselves from patronizing foreign employees and instead pursue the autocratic leadership roles.

Leadership at the Middle Management and Supervisory Levels

At the middle management and supervisory levels, both Chinese local companies and Japanese subsidiaries are largely autocratic in their leadership styles. More specifically, 9 of the 11 local companies and 5 of the 7 Japanese subsidiaries are in this category of leadership. Also, an increasing number of American subsidiaries adopt the autocratic style at middle management and supervisory levels. Many American chief executives underscore the difficulties in indoctrinating

[10] *Ibid.*, p. 5.
[11] *Ibid.*, p. 205.
[12] Kazue Kitagawa, "A View of Modern Management in Japan," *Management Japan*, Vol. 3, No. 4, 1970, p. 21.

local personnel at these levels to utilize the consultative type of leadership.

It is interesting to note in Table 5-1, however, that two local and two Japanese subsidiaries utilize the consultative leadership style at all levels of management. This, indeed, reflects both an over-all company orientation toward employees and the adoption of American management styles. As might be expected, these particular companies are not only competitive in international markets but also highly successful financially.

TABLE 5-1. *Leadership Styles at Three Managerial Levels in Taiwan*

Leadership Style	Managerial Levels Top Level			Middle Level			Supervisory Level		
	A	C	J	A	C	J	A	C	J
Consultative	6	2	2	5	2	2	4	2	2
Autocratic	3	1	4	4	9	4	5	9	5
Bureaucratic-autocratic		1	1			1			
Paternalistic-autocratic		7							

A = American Subsidiaries (n = 9)
C = Chinese Local Companies (n = 11)
J = Japanese Subsidiaries (n = 7)

Leader's Perception of Subordinates' Abilities

As data in Table 5-2 illustrate, Japanese and Chinese leaders seem to have much less confidence and trust in their subordinates than their American counterparts in Taiwan. Both Japanese and Chinese managers feel that subordinates need close watching and guidance and should not be left to function on their own. In contrast, American managers place much emphasis on training subordinates at all levels and place greater confidence and trust in their abilities.

To be sure, not all Chinese personnel working for American subsidiaries fully comprehend the real meaning of the attitude displayed in American leadership style. Quite a few are skeptical about the true intentions of American managers. As a result, some American managers express their feelings of frustration by applying the leadership concept practiced in their parent companies in the United States. On the other hand, managers in a few of the Chinese firms, as well as those in the American companies in Taiwan, are quite confident and satisfied to adopt democratic or consultative leadership styles in their operations; their subordinates, especially the young, Western educated personnel, seem to prefer this type of managerial style.

TABLE 5-2. *Leaders' Perceptions of Subordinates' Abilities*

Leaders' Perceptions	Managerial Levels Top Level			Middle Level			Supervisory Level		
	A	C	J	A	C	J	A	C	J
a. Placed much confidence in subordinates	6	4		5	3	1	5	1	1
b. Placed some confidence in subordinates	2	4	6	2	4	4	2	3	2
c. Placed no confidence in subordinates	1	3	1	2	4	2	2	7	4

A = American subsidiaries (n = 9)
C = Chinese local companies (n = 11)
J = Japanese subsidiaries (n = 7)

Managerial Attitudes

The prevailing paternalistic leadership flavor in Taiwan was also brought out in the questionnaire survey of American subsidiaries (n = 23) and local Chinese companies (n = 76). In this survey we asked a series of direct and indirect questions to ascertain managerial attitudes on many aspects of management, including the leadership role.

As Table 5-3 shows, 70 per cent of the American and the Chinese executives responding to the survey agree that human relations in Taiwan have an authoritarian and paternalistic flavor. It is interesting to note that a very small fraction of these managers disagreed with this contention.

Similarly, the large majority of both the American (57 percent) and Chinese executives (49 per cent) feel that the average human being prefers to be directed, wishes to avoid responsibility, and has relatively little ambition. In other words, these executives seem to have much less confidence and trust in the abilities and aspirations of their employees. Many of these executives also feel that leadership traits and abilities are basically inborn and cannot be acquired by everyone. In fact,

TABLE 5-3. *Managers' Attitudes on Leadership Role in American and Local Companies in Taiwan (Questionnaire Survey)*

Questions	U.S. Subsidiaries n = 23			Local Companies n = 76		
	Agree (%)	Dis-agree (%)	No Answer (%)	Agree (%)	Dis-agree (%)	No Answer (%)
The human relations in Taiwan have an authoritarian and paternalistic flavor.	70	4	26	70	13	17
While democratic style of management sounds good on paper, in order to accomplish company goals year after year, top executives have to be assertive and dominate the views and thinking of other lower-level executives.	61	30	9	40	40	20
In a work situation, if the subordinates cannot influence me, then I lose some influence on them.	48	26	26	40	38	22
Chinese executives communicate less to the "middle manager" than American executives and thereby save "executive time."	35	43	22	34	50	16
The average human being prefers to be directed, wishes to avoid responsibility and has relatively little ambition.	57	39	4	49	27	24
Leadership skills can be acquired by most people regardless of their particular inborn traits and abilities.	17	78	5	43	45	12

there are more American executives (78 per cent) than Chinese managers (45 per cent) who feel this way.

A large majority of the American (61 per cent) and Chinese executives (40 per cent) also believe that the democratic style of management sounds good on paper but that, in order to achieve the company's goals, the executive must be assertive and dominate the views and thinking of lower level managers. To recall, however, executives interviewed in American subsidiaries in Taiwan do not seem to feel this way. In fact (Table 5-1), six of the nine U.S. subsidiaries utilize the consultative type of leadership.

In related questions concerning the communication patterns utilized by managers and the perceived influence of subordinates on executives, more than one third of the American and Chinese executives feel that top Chinese executives communicate less to middle managers than do top level American executives. Forty eight per cent of the American executives and 40 per cent of the Chinese managers prefer interacting influences among subordinates and superordinates.

Interpretation of Survey Results

Results of the questionnaire survey indicate some conflicting attitudes. On one hand, we find confirmation of the prevailing paternalistic leadership style and philosophy in industrial enterprises in Taiwan. This is especially clear in responses to questions one, two, and five, outlined in Table 5-3. On the other hand, we also find American executives demonstrating less faith in the democratic style of leadership. This is particularly evident from the responses to questions two, five, and six. At the same time, we also see Chinese executives having second thoughts on the desirability of a paternalistic-autocratic style of leadership. They tend to swing to the other side of the pendulum and opt for a democratic style of leadership or at least agree in principle to such a leadership role.

In contrast to the survey results, the companies studied through the intensive interview method show some definite patterns; American subsidiaries utilize consultative or democratic leadership style at the top level, while Japanese and Chinese managers are paternalistic and autocratic respectively.

One would ask: Why are there conflicting results? We are inclined to believe that the interview analyses reflect the actual leadership styles, while results obtained from the questionnaire survey show managerial attitudes toward the leadership role. The small size of our interview sample notwithstanding (n = 27), we feel that differences in the two research results indicate differences between managerial attitudes and managerial practices. In other words, managerial attitudes are not consistent with their practices.

Managerial practices are on-going phenomena and appropriate managerial attitudes must develop before managerial practices can be changed. If we interpret our survey results in this light, we can say that managerial attitudes are in a state of flux. That is, the Chinese executives are having doubts about the desirability of paternalistic leadership style and are showing some interest in adopting consultative or democratic styles, while American executives desire adoption of the prevailing paternalistic-autocratic style. In other words, these results show interacting influences at work in a cross-cultural setting where each counterpart is giving a closer look at the other's managerial system or style.

Leadership Styles: International Comparisons

Results obtained in the previous study undertaken in Argentina,

TABLE 5-4. *Leadership Styles: International Comparisons**

	U.S. Subsidiaries	Local Companies
ARGENTINA-BRAZIL-URUGUAY	n = 20	n = 17
Democratic	13	6
Authoritarian	5	8
Bureaucratic	1	1
Not clear-cut	1	2
INDIA	n = 17	n = 17
Democratic	7	3
Authoritarian	4	9
Bureaucratic	6	5
PHILIPPINES	n = 10	n = 11
Democratic	3	4
Authoritarian	7	6
Bureaucratic	–	1

* Adopted from Anant R. Negandhi and S. B. Prasad, *Comparative Management* (New York: Appleton-Century-Crofts, 1971). Permission of the publisher is greatfully acknowledged.

Brazil, India, the Philippines, and Uruguay[13] show patterns of leadership style similar to those used in Taiwan. That is, in these five developing countries, we also found a larger number of American subsidiaries opting for consultative or democratic leadership style, compared to their local counterparts which preferred autocratic or bureaucratic style. As can be seen in Table 5-4, 23 of the 47 American subsidiaries utilize democratic leadership style compared to 13 of the 45 local firms.

The paternalistic outlook or philosophy is much less in vogue in India and the Philippines than what we observed in Taiwan, especially among the local firms.

Is Leadership Style Culture-Bound?

In recent years, a growing number of scholars conducting management studies in developing countries have attempted to demonstrate that the leadership style in those countries is authoritarian or paternalistic in nature. For example studies by Harbison and Myers,[14] Haire, Ghiselli, and Porter,[15] Meade,[16] and a number of research reports by the Management Research Center at the University of Rochester[17] confirm this contention. Our findings in Taiwan and other developing countries support thiscontention.

However, many cross-cultural management researchers have further advocated that the consultative or democratic model so widely used in the United States may not be preferable for other countries, especially developing societies. Meade,[18] for example, who replicated the Lippitt and White study,[19] showed that in India, morale and productivity are higher under authoritarian style than under demo-

[13] See A. R. Negandhi and S. B. Prasad, *Comparative Management* (New York: Appleton-Century-Crofts, 1971), pp. 67-77.

[14] Harbison and Myers, *op. cit.*

[15] M. Haire, D. E. Ghiselli, and L. W. Porter, *Managerial Thinking: An International Study* (New York: John Wiley, 1966).

[16] R. D. Meade, "An Experimental Study of Leadership in India," *Journal of Social Psychology*, LXXII (1967), pp. 35-43.

[17] G. V. Barrett and B. M. Bass, "Comparative Surveys of Managerial Attitudes and Behavior," in *Comparative Management: Teaching, Research and Ttraining*, ed. by J. Boddewyn (New York: Graduate School of Business Administration, 1970), pp. 179-207.

[18] Meade, *op. cit.*

[19] R. Lippitt and R. K. White, "An Experimental Study of Leadership and Group Life," in E. E. Macroby, *et. al.* (eds.), *Readings in Social Psychology* (3rd edition; New York: Holt, 1958).

cratic leadership. These results are a reversal of the Lippitt and White findings concerning the United States.

In their recent paper, Professors Barrett and Bass, after reviewing a number of management studies undertaken in foreign countries, arrive at these conclusions:

> There are differences among countries in preferred styles of leadership. These differences in leadership styles appear to be largely culturally based and at this point in time it would be naive to advocate one model of leadership style as being optimum for all cultural groups. The wide-advocated American model of participative management may not be optimum for all cultures and in fact may be disfunctional in some.[20]

In light of our research studies and experience in some dozen developing countries, we find such remarks somewhat disturbing. Although we do subscribe to the viewpoint that there are specific cultural patterns found in each country and that the leadership role is conceived through the cultural heritage, we neither accept that the prevailing style of leadership in developing countries is the most appropriate, nor do we think that a specific style is unchangeable.

On the contrary, we found a sizeable number of American and local firms in Argentina, Brazil, Chile, Greece, India, the Philippines, Taiwan, and Uruguay utilize a consultative type of leadership in their operations. These firms are not necessarily less effective than those utilizing authoritarian or paternalistic styles. As a matter of fact, we found the former companies more effective and growth oriented. It is true that a number of authoritarian or bureaucratic organizations we studied are also making huge profits. We contend, however, that their profit-making ability is a function of market conditions (seller's market) rather than their leadership style.

Indeed, a leader does play an important and crucial role in the survival and growth of an organization. Yet, in this modern era, complex industrial organizations depend not only on their leaders but on the total human and capital resources they possess. Particularly in recent years, the role of human resources has been increasingly recognized.

The next chapter analyzes the various aspects of human-resource management.

[20] Barrett and Bass, *op. cit.*, p. 194.

CHAPTER VI

MANPOWER MANAGEMENT

Introduction

Of all the factors, the management of human resources is the most critical. As Likert has stated: "of all the tasks of management, managing the human components is the central and most important task, because all else depends upon how well it is done."[1]

A similar view is also echoed by Mr. Kumazawa, President of Oji Paper Company of Japan:

> ..., Human resources should be properly shown in figures as assets on the balance sheet just as physical assets are, as an indication of corporate strength ... Cultivation of human resources offer a scope of promise vastly wider than that of physical resources.[2]

In recent years, a growing number of nations are systematically undertaking manpower planning to increase their potential for rapid economic growth. Taiwan's own concern for the development of human resources at a national level is reflected in the organization of a special Manpower Development Committee in the Council for International Economic Cooperation and Development (CIECD). This committee is charged with the responsibilities of examining, in detail, the problems of education, training, recruitment, distribution, motivation, and utilization of the labor force for economic development in Taiwan.

At the micro(organizational) level, many business organizations, as

[1] Rensis Likert, *The Human Organization: Its Management and Value* (New York: McGraw Hill Book Company, Inc., 1967), p. 1.

[2] Sadao Kumazawa, "Future Management – Effective Use of Human Resources," *Management Japan* (July-September, 1967), p. 5.

well as the governmental agencies in the United States, have paid considerable attention to manpower policies and planning, recruitment, selection procedures, appraisal techniques, and training programs. This has been particularly true since the depression years of the 1930's. Many testing devices – psychological and otherwise – have been developed for selecting employees and matching individual abilities with job requirements. Recent trends among large-scale U.S. corporations suggest an attempt to utilize such "management science" concepts as mathematical, statistical, and operations research models for the personnel function – e.g., recruiting, selecting, testing, performance evaluation, and training.[3]

Purpose of this Chapter

This chapter will analyze the various aspects of manpower management practices observed in the Taiwan companies. Data for the following factors were collected for this study:

a. Manpower policies
b. Organization of personnel functions
c. Job analysis
d. Selection procedure and criteria
e. Promotion and appraisal systems
f. Training programs
g. Compensation and motivation devices
h. Environmental factors affecting manpower management

A brief description of manpower management practices being utilized by American parent companies in the United States will provide a comparative perspective.

MANPOWER MANAGEMENT IN 15 U.S. PARENT COMPANIES

Manpower Policies

A large majority of the U.S. parent companies studied (12 out of the 15) have formulated specific manpower policies. Many of these policies cover such concern as how to create an atmosphere where the individual participant can contribute to the fullest of his abilities, and

[3] See Paul S. Greenlaw and Robert D. Smith, *Personnel Management: A Management Science Approach* (Scranton, Pennsylvania: International Textbook Company, 1970).

how to select the right individuals for the required positions. Particularly, the chief executives and the top-level executive committees pay considerable attention to the formulation of manpower policies.

In all parent companies, implementing manpower policies is undertaken by the personnel department. Each department is, itself, well organized and has many divisions, such as management training and development, wage and salary administration, employee services, fringe benefits, etc. These companies pay particular attention to the

TABLE 6-1. *Aspects of Manpower Management and Personnel Practices in the 15 U.S. Parent Companies*

Items	Number of Companies
Formal manpower policies	13
Organization of personnel function as separate department	15
Major Divisions within the Personnel Department	
Wage and salary adm. division	15
Employee services division	12
Fringe benefits division	10
Training division	14
Management training division	12
Manpower policy group	6
Industrial relations and employee relations division	15
Major Personnel Practices	
Formalized job description and evaluation	14
Formalized employee selection and appraisal	14
Employee testing devices	14
Formal dismissal and layoff status	10
Development of selection and promotion criteria	10
Formalized employee health and safety programs	14
Formalized employee recreation and vacation programs	10
Retirement schemes	9
Wage and salary surveys	10
Employee suggestion systems	15
Development of management succession charts and management inventory	9
Supervisory training programs	14
Blue-collar employee training programs	14
Management training programs	12

training and development of employees at all levels. Of course, companies utilize varied types and forms of training methods at different levels. These include on-the-job training, formal training within and outside the firm, and job rotation within the firm and its subsidiaries or division. Few of these firms utilize behavioral researchers from universities to conduct their management training. More than half of the parent companies prepare elaborate management succession charts and management inventory. On an average, these firms spend one to five per cent of the company's working hours in providing training at various levels. This represents an expenditure ranging from 5 to 15 per cent of the firms' gross sales.

Holden and his co-researchers found a similar trend among 15 large-scale U.S. companies. For example, they report that:

> The identification and planned development of key personnel has become a vital part of the total long-range planning activity in all the 15 corporations. ... Replacement charts, backup lists, and individual development plans for each executive position are the rule rather than the exception today.[4]

Table 6-1 shows the various aspects of manpower management and personnel practices observed in the 15 U.S. parent companies studied by us.

MANPOWER MANAGEMENT POLICIES OF COMPANIES IN TAIWAN

Of the 27 companies studied in Taiwan, less than half spell out specific manpower policies. Among the three sets of companies (U.S. subsidiary, Japanese subsidiary, and local firms), Japanese subsidiaries are the most diffuse about their policies on human resources; only one of these subsidiaries has specific policies. In contrast, 5 of the 9 U.S. subsidiaries and 5 of the 11 local firms document their manpower policies.

The underlying concerns reflected in these manpower policies are to satisfy the employee's needs, to achieve higher organizational effectiveness, to select the right individuals, and to avoid the "trouble makers" in the organization.

[4] P. E. Holden, *et al.*, *Top Management* (New York: McGraw Hill Book Company, Inc., 1968), p. 208.

A majority of the companies with documented policies arrive at such policies through a consultative process. That is, policies are formulated by the executive committee rather than the top executive or the owner himself.

TABLE 6-2. *Manpower Policies: Formulation, Objectives, and Decision-Making*

Manpower Policies	U.S. Subsidiary (n = 9)	Japanese Subsidiary (n = 7)	Local Firm (n = 11)
Formally Stated:			
Yes	5	1	5
No	4	6	6
Objectives of Manpower Policies			
a. To satisfy the employee's needs and to achieve higher organizational effectiveness	4		2
b. To select right individuals	1	2	1
c. To avoid trouble-makers			2
d. No specific objectives	4	5	6
Decision Making Concerning Manpower Policies			
Top executive/owner	1	1	1
Executive committee	4	–	3
Ad-hoc basis	4	6	7

Organization of Personnel Function

A company's concern for preserving and developing its human resources can be discerned from its method of organizing the personnel function and the hierarchical place and status attributed to that department.

Our research inquiry and data, reported in Table 6-3, indicate a dismal picture regarding the company's concern for human resources. Their personnel function is not considered very important or even mildly important in many of the Taiwan companies. Only 4 of the 27 firms (3 U.S. subsidiaries and one local firm) organize a personnel department separately with qualified personnel. Two additional companies (one U.S. subsidiary and one local firm) have a separately organized personnel department with semi-qualified personnel. In the remaining companies (21 of the 27), the top executive and/or the owner, or the production manager oversees the personnel function.

TABLE 6-3. *Organization of Personnel Department*

How is the Personnel Dept. Organized?	U.S. Subsidiary (n = 9)	Japanese Subsidiary (n = 7)	Local Firm (n = 11)
Separately organized with qualified personnel	3	0	1
Separately organized with not-so-qualified personnel	1	0	1
Not separately organized-plant manager, general manager, and owner in charge	5	7	9

Personnel Practices in Taiwan

Notwithstanding a lack of sophistication in formulating manpower policies and organizing the personnel function, a firm needs to carry out personnel activities which concern recruiting, selecting, training, and developing, and place the individual employee to his specific task. A company must also be concerned with compensating and motivating employees. How well these functions are organized and executed will, to a large extent, determine the survival, growth, and profitability of the industrial enterprise.

As noted earlier, the U.S. parent companies we studied, as well as the large-scale U.S. companies researched by other authors, suggest a great deal of systematic effort in undertaking these activities. (See Table 6-1).

Specific personnel practices discussed in the following sections are:

a. Job analysis (description, specification, and evaluation)
b. Selection procedures and criteria
c. Promotion and appraisal systems
d. Training and development programs
e. Compensation and motivation devices used

Tables 6-4 through 6-7 provide a comparative profile of personnel activities undertaken by the American subsidiaries, Japanese subsidiaries, and local companies in Taiwan. Let us examine these data in more detail.

Job Analysis

Regarding the personnel function, management's very initial task is to gather, analyze, and record information on the duties, responsibilities, and qualifications that are required of individuals performing given tasks. In the personnel management literature, these types of activities are subsumed under *Job Analysis.* Briefly, this function is composed of two interrelated activities: (a) *Job description* which records the principal duties, responsibilites, and activities involved in specific jobs, and (b) *Job specification* which outlines personal qualifications the individual must possess in order to perform the assigned tasks in a specific job position.[5]

As can be seen from Table 6-4, only American subsidiaries are articulate in carrying out this function. Specifically, 6 of the 9 American subsidiaries, as compared to 2 of the 11 local firms, and none of the Japanese subsidiaries, formalize such activities. The personnel departments and/or the time and motion departments are responsible for undertaking these activities.

As reported in Chapter 4, the Japanese companies are structured in collective organizational units and the importance placed on individual positions is minimal. This is borne out by their lack of concern for such activities as job description and job specification. By and large, local companies in Taiwan (except 2 of the 11) also follow the Japanese rather than the American style.

Job Evaluation

Job evaluation or an employee appraisal system is practiced in some form or another by a majority of the American and Japanese subsidiaries. Specifically, 7 of the 9 American subsidiaries, all of the 7 Japanese counterparts, and 3 of the 11 local firms use standardized rating forms and/or periodic reports from immediate supervisors to evaluate employee performance. Among the American subsidiaries such devices are used for all levels of employees. However, in the Japanese

[5] For more detailed treatment see H. J. Chruden and A. W. Sherman, Jr., *Personnel Management* (Cincinnati: South-Western Publishing Company, 1959), pp. 455-480.

and local firms these practices are restricted to blue-collar workers only. The Japanese utilization of an appraisal system, at least for blue-collar employees, reflects, to some extent, a "competitive war" between Japanese and American companies in Taiwan as they compete for world markets. As pointed out elsewhere,[6] in order to recapture lost markets in the United States, many American companies have gone to Taiwan and other developing countries primarily to reduce labor cost. The Japanese companies have followed the Americans and opened subsidiaries in Taiwan to reduce their own labor cost. Their interest in utilizing some sort of an appraisal system for blue-collar employees is simply to gain some perspective on the cost-productivity ratios.

Selection and Promotion

Management's concern to treat human resources as a critical input in the functioning of an organization also can be discerned by looking at a firm's selection and promotion procedures and criteria.

As noted earlier, considerable attention is paid to these activities in the United States. Among the 15 U.S. parent companies participating in our study, we particularly noted that systematic attempts are made to develop objective criteria and procedures for selecting and promoting employees at all levels.

As can be seen from Table 6-4, the selection of executive and supervisory personnel is not regarded as "high priority" by many of the Japanese and local companies. The majority of the American subsidiaries, in contrast, pay considerable attention to selecting individuals for these positions.

However, all three sets of companies pay very cursory attention to the selection and recruitment of blue-collar employees. The blue-collar selection procedure used by a few of the local companies amounts to no more than sending a truck to a nearby village and picking up anybody with arms, feet, and eyes who is ready to work on anything. These particular firms also consistently employ boys and girls below 14 years of age who are otherwise forbidden to work under the labor laws in Taiwan. It must be stressed, however, that such practices are

[6] A. R. Negandhi, "New Frontiers for American Business: A Case Study of Investment Climate in Taiwan," *California Management Review* (Fall, 1971), pp. 96-102.

not very common among the majority of the local firms, and none of the American and Japanese subsidiaries appear to violate these "child labor" law provisions. Nevertheless, their practices for recruiting and selecting blue-collar employees are far from sophisticated.

Turning to selection and promotion criteria, American subsidiaries consider education and training more important. A majority of the Japanese subsidiaries and local firms regard age (seniority), experience, and family and market ties as more important criteria for selecting and promoting employees.

Particularly, the regard for age and seniority as promotion criteria, is much more common among the local firms. This was vividly borne out in a questionnaire survey of 23 U.S. subsidiaries and 76 local firms. One of the questions asked: "Does seniority of the management personnel outweigh their managerial ability as a basis for promotion and higher compensation?" Forty-nine per cent of the local companies, in contrast to 14 per cent of the U.S. subsidiaries, replied in the affirmative. Thirty-two per cent of the U.S. subsidiaries and only 4 per cent of the local companies indicated that "this will never occur in their organizations."

By and large, the American subsidiaries follow the practice of recruiting managerial and supervisory personnel from outside sources. Japanese and local firms seek these personnel from within the organization.

Impact of the Confucian Philosophy

Reverence for age and seniority and its corresponding managerial practices of the permanent employment system and seniority-based reward system found in Taiwan, Japan, China and other oriental countries, largely stem from the heritage of Confucianism.[7]

Confucianism, of course, stresses benevolence, propriety, wisdom, and obedience. Translated into actual management practices, these virtues give rise to collectivism, particularistic, and situation-centered orientations. Under the particularistic orientation, the manager is incapable of resisting pressure from his primary group. As Mr. Yang stated:

[7] For further elaboration on this point, see M. Y. Yoshino, *Japan's Managerial System* (Cambridge: M.I.T. Press, 1968), pp. 1-18.

His (manager-bureaucrat) personal primary group was his permanent base of social life, the society from which he sprang, which he brought with him when he entered officialism, and to which he must return when his official career comes to an end.[8]

The situation-centered characteristic of the Chinese manager is contrasted with the American counterparts by Mr. Hsu in these words:

Int he American way of life the emphasis is placed upon the predilection of the individual, a characteristic we shall call 'individual-centered' ... Being individual centered, the American moves toward social and psychological isolation ... being situation-centered, the Chinese is inclined to be socially or psychologically dependent on others.[9]

Notwithstanding such cultural differences among the American, Japanese, and Chinese managers, we are inclined to believe that in the dynamic industrial age in which we live, more and more decisions are based on practical realities rather than traditions. For example, Marsh and Mannis have challenged the concept of the Japanese employee's lifetime commitment to the firm. Their findings indicate that:

... Two interpretations of lifetime commitment suggested by Abeggdlen and others, one – status enhancement – is supported empirically but is not unique to Japan; the other – moral loyalty to the company as such – would be unique if it existed, but there is no evidence that it does exist apart from status enhancement. As Japan reaches higher levels of modernization, a complex of forces impinges upon lifetime commitment.[10]

Our study also seems to indicate that the economic and market conditions in Taiwan explain a great deal of their lack of sophistication in manpower policies and practices. We shall discuss this point in some detail at the end of this chapter. Let us look now at the type of training programs existing in the three sets of companies in Taiwan.

Training

Training programs of some sort are organized in about one-half of the companies studied. Particularly, on-the-job training for blue-collar

[8] C. K. Yang, "Some Characteristics of Chinese Bureaucratic Behavior," *The Confucianism in Action*, ed. by D. S. Nivison and A. F. Wright (Palo Alto: Stanford University Press, 1950), p. 158.

[9] Francis L. K. Hsu, *American and Chinese: Two Ways of Life* (New York: Aberlard-Schurman, 1953), p. 10.

[10] Robert M. Marsh and Hiroshi Mannari, "Lifetime Commitment in Japan: Rules, Norms and Values," *American Journal of Sociology*, Vol. 76, No. 5, p. 811.

employees is most popular among the Japanese and local firms. However, only 3 of the 27 companies (2 U.S. and 1 Japanese) utilize formal (in-company or outside) training programs for their operators.

For their managerial and supervisory personnel, 9 of the 27 companies utilize formal training programs. Here, also, the American subsidiaries provide the lead. This can be seen from data presented in Table 6-5.

In recent years, realizing the need for managerial talent in the economic and industrial development in Taiwan, a number of governmental and semi-governmental agencies have started various types of management training programs. A couple of leading universities, such as the National Taiwan University and the National Cheng-Chi University, have instituted graduate programs in business and public administration. In addition, a number of associations and productivity councils offer short management training programs. Our research indicates, however, that while the American subsidiaries are quite active in both contributing to and utilizing these facilities, many of the Japanese and local firms are not.

The systematic development of human resources, particularly at the managerial level, is considered by many scholars and governmental officials to be a necessary high priority in achieving rapid economic and industrial development. However, our inquiries indicate a pessimistic outlook in this matter. In other words, not many companies in Taiwan pay much attention to management training and development.

TABLE 6-4. *Personnel Practices in Taiwan*

Type of Personnel Practice		U.S. Subsidiary (n = 9)	Japanese Subsidiary (n = 7)	Local Firm (n = 11)
Job Analysis: Description and Specification				
Formally done	yes	6	0	2
	no	3	7	9
Who is Responsible for these Activities				
Personnel department		3		
Time and motion study		3		1
Supervisor				1
No one/not done		3	7	9

TABLE 6-4 (*continued*)

Type of Personnel Practice	U.S. Subsidiary (n = 9)	Japanese Subsidiary (n = 7)	Local Firm (n = 11)
Selection of Executives and Supervisors			
Procedure			
Intensive interview by the executive committee	3	0	1
Intensive interview by personnel/or functional managers	3	1	
Simple questionnaire	2	5	2
Ad-hoc basis-depending upon the immediate needs and whims of the supervisor	1	1	8
Selection Criteria for Executive and Supervisory Personnel			
Education and training	9	1	2
Experience and age		4	5
Market contacts		2	1
Family ties			3
Promotion Criteria for Executive and Supervisory Personnel			
Education and training	6	2	2
Length of service and age	2	4	6
Aggressiveness		1	1
Loyalty to company	1		2
For Other Employees			
Education and training	7	2	2
Length of service		3	5
Ability to get along with others	2		
Technical ability		2	3
Ad-hoc/not clear			1
Appraisal System			
Standardized forms	4	4	2
Periodic reports from the immediate supervisor	3	3	1
Ad-hoc/informal system	2		8

TABLE 6-4 (*continued*)

Type of Personnel Practice	U.S. Subsidiary (n = 9)	Japanese Subsidiary (n = 7)	Local Firm (n = 11)
Training Programs at Various Levels			
Blue-collar worker			
yes	5	4	4
no	4	3	7
Supervisor			
yes	5	1	1
no	4	6	10
Management personnel			
yes	4	1	2
no	5	6	9
Percentage of the Total Company Man Hours Spent on Training (estimated by interviewees)			
16% to 20%			1
11% to 15%	1		
5% to 10%	3	1	
Less than 5%	5	5	8
None		1	2

Compensation and Motivation

One of the most perplexing questions for the manager of any organization is how to motivate employees to work diligently at a peak level. In industrialized countries, various schemes have been practiced for motivating employees. These practices range from simple monetary compensation to the more advanced techniques geared to satisfy higher levels of human needs in terms of self-actualization and esteem.

Although researchers disagree about the exact ranking of human needs, there is a consensus among scholars that basic physiological needs and the need for security or safety are at the top of any needs-hierarchy. Maslow,[11] for example, has proposed the following hierarchy of human needs which has received wide acceptance:

1. Basic physiological needs (food, water, clothing, shelter, air, etc.).

[11] Abraham Maslow, *Motivation and Personality* (New York: Harper and Brothers, 1954).

TABLE 6-5. *Types of Training Programs at Various Levels*

	on-the-job	formal-in-company	formal outside	on the job plus formal-in-company	on the job plus formal outside	job rotation	ad-hoc basis
U.S. Subsidiary							
Managerial personnel				2	2		5
Supervisor				4	1		4
Operator	2			1	1	1	4
Japanese Subsidiary							
Managerial personnel					1		6
Supervisor				1			6
Operator	3			1			3
Local Firm							
Managerial personnel	1				1		9
Supervisor				1			10
Operator	4						7

2. Security or safety for the continuation of physiological needs.
3. Love or desire for affection and association with others.
4. Esteem or self-assertion.
5. Self-actualization or self-fulfillment.

Data collected from the firms in this study indicate that most of these companies rely on monetary compensation to motivate their employees. Although the Japanese and local firms appear to stress the importance of their employees' security and socio-psychological needs, we observed no specific management practices in these firms which seemed to satisfy such needs.

To repeat, many of the Japanese and local companies pursue a permanent employment policy. However, this policy by itself is inadequate in satisfying the higher level needs of self-actualization, self-esteem, or ego-fulfillment. Many employees interviewed in these companies indicate the lack of satisfaction of these needs.

In terms of types of compensation, the salary plus an annual bonus are most popular among all three sets of companies. This is shown in Table 6-6.

TABLE 6-6. *Compensation at Various Levels*

	Types of Compensation			
	Hourly Wage	Hourly Wages plus Bonus	Salary	Salary plus Bonus
Levels				
U.S. subsidiary				
Management			5	4
Clerical			3	6
Blue-collar employee	1		1	7
Japanese subsidiary				
Management			1	6
Clerical			1	6
Blue-collar employee			1	6
Local firm				
Management			4	7
Clerical			4	7
Blue-collar employee	5	2	2	2

International Comparisons on Manpower Management

Manpower management practices observed in other developing countries[12] (Argentina, Brazil, India, the Philippines, Uruguay) provide the opportunity for making certain international comparisons.

Data on formulating manpower policies suggest some differences between U.S. subsidiaries and the local firms. For example, 8 of the 17 U.S. subsidiaries in India and 12 of the 17 local Indian companies have formally stated policies. In contrast, only 5 of the 20 U.S. subsidiaries, and 5 of the 17 local companies in Latin America seem to have formalized policies. In the Philippines, the proportion is still less. Only 3 of the 10 U.S. subsidiaries and only 1 of the 11 local companies formliazed these policies.

Data from the companies in Taiwan (Table 6-2) suggest that the U.S. subsidiaries in Taiwan are more like their Indian counterparts, whereas the Japanese subsidiaries and local Taiwan firms are more similar to the local companies in Latin America and the Philippines.

Similarly, selection and promotion procedures are well articulated in a majority of the U.S. subsidiaries; less than half of the local firms studied (n = 47) in the five developing countries have established selection and promotion procedures. Training and development schemes are widely prevalent among U.S. subsidiaries in India and the Philippines. Sizable local companies in India and the Philippines also have formalized training programs. On the other hand, in Argentina, Brazil, and Uruguay, training and development are on an informal, ad-hoc basis. Thus, in respect to training programs, we find the companies in Taiwan more closely resemble those in India and the Philippines.

In regard to compensation and motivation devices, neither U.S. subsidiaries nor local companies in any of the five countries differ significantly from the companies in Taiwan. Primarily, these companies use monetary rewards for blue-collar workers. Here, also, American subsidiaries attempt to pay higher wages than do the local firms in all of these countries, including Taiwan.

To recap, comparing manpower management practices in Taiwan with those observed in five other developing countries places the Taiwan firms somewhere between companies in the Philippines and

[12] See A. R. Negandhi and S. B. Prasad, *Comparative Management* (New York: Appleton-Century-Crofts, 1971), especially pp. 51-58.

those in the Latin American countries. Both the U.S. subsidiaries and the local companies in India seem to have more advanced manpower practices than those in Taiwan.

Environmental Factors Affecting Manpower Management Practices in Developing Countries

The preceding analysis of data concerning manpower management practices in the six developing countries clearly suggests that the majority of the local companies do not utilize human resources in the most efficient manner. On the other hand, economic planners, as well as government officials and politicians, are not only aware of but ardently advocate the importance of human resources in stimulating economic and industrial developments. Also, there is visible evidence at the macro-level (national and governmental levels) suggesting a concern for developing and utilizing human resources to this end. This concern at the macro-level is readily reflected in various institutes, councils, and training schools being formulated by the governments of these countries. Some governments have even formulated a cabinet-level ministry of manpower development. In other words, there seems to be proper awareness of the importance of human resources at the macro-level; the corresponding concern for these resources at the micro-level (firm-level) is utterly lacking. Needless to say, the reader is prompted to ask why this is so. While we do not pretend to have the final answer to this question, we did inquire into this problem. During our interviews with executives, governmental officials, and university professors in Taiwan and the other five developing countries, two environmental factors were mentioned frequently. These were: (a) abundance of labor supply, and (b) market conditions. Let us analyze these two factors with respect to Taiwan.

Abundance of Labor Supply

Quantitatively, the supply of manpower in Taiwan is abundant. Statistics computed on the basis of the 1964 Census give the following breakdown of available human resources in Taiwan.

Various labor surveys taken in recent years also indicate that the rate of participation in employment is on the decrease while the rate of potential labor is on the increase. Household statistics show that because of population growth and a lack of employment opportunities among the age group over 12, the potential labor force has increased.

TABLE 6-7. *Human Resources in Taiwan (1964 Census)*

Unit 1,000 Persons

Age Bracket	Percentage of total Population	Number of Persons
1-14	45.5	5,572
15-59	50.1	6,148
over 60	4.4	537

Source: *A Brief Report on the Supply of Labor in Taiwan* (Taipei: Taiwan Industrial Development and Investment Center, 1967), p. 2.

Concurrently, participation in employment has decreased. For example, of the 2.2 million added to the labor force during the years 1958-1968, only 729,440 or one-third found jobs.[13]

This situation in the labor supply does create an overall impression that the labor force is plentiful in Taiwan. Because of this abundant labor market, many executives are of the opinion that it is unnecessary to spend time and money training and developing employees. This attitude may be justifiable in the short-run; yet, when one looks at the future needs of an economy, serious questions arise.

Taiwan's Fourth Economic Development Plan, for example, anticipates the following increase in demand for the various categories of skills.

As the table shows, the demand for skilled workers, technicians, and administrative personnel will increase substantively beyond 1970 and the industrial firms will find it difficult to obtain needed man power. As a matter of fact, during our interviews in 1968 many executives complained about the short supply of trained workers and technical and managerial personnel.

Market Situation in Taiwan

Another factor that seems responsible for the lack of sophistication in manpower management practices in Taiwan is the nature of market conditions. Most of the developing countries are experiencing seller's market conditions. Taiwan, too, has a seller's market for many consumer-durable products. However, she also has extremely com-

[13] "Problems and Prospects of Manpower Resources in the Republic of China," *Economic Review* (Taipei, Taiwan), No. 126 (November-December, 1968), p. 16.

TABLE 6-8. *New Employees Needed in Period Covered by Taiwan's Fourth Economic Development Plan (1965-1970)*

Unit 1,000 Persons

Category Number	Classification of Professions	Employees in 1970	Employees in 1965	Number Increased	Retirements & Deaths in 5 Yrs. (Ratio 7.8%)	New Employees Needed in 5 Yrs.	New Employees Needed Each Yr.
0-9		4,624	3,830	794	299	1,093	219
0	Specialists & technicians	187	146	41	11	52	10
1	Administrative personnel	131	98	33	8	41	8
2	Assistant administrative personnel	266	208	58	16	74	15
3	Sales & procurement personnel	510	398	112	31	143	29
4	Farmers, fishermen, lumbermen, etc.	1,950	1,801	149	141	290	58
5	Miners & masons	79	67	12	5	17	3
6	Transportation & communication workers	160	125	35	10	45	9
7/8	Technical workers & workers not belonging to other categories	1,076	799	279	61	358	72
9	Sports & recreational personnel	265	208	57	16	73	15

Source: "Problems and Prospectus of Manpower Resources in The Republic of China," *Economic Review*, Nov.-Dec. 1968, p. 17.

petitive markets for selected consumer products, such as drugs and textiles.

Firms facing seller's market conditions have become quite insensitive to unit-cost and worker-efficiency. In contrast, firms facing a competitive market are extremely cautious about money expended on training and developing employees. They are worried about their future. In both instances, executives prefer to take short-range perspectives and attempt to "save" unnecessary expenditures on developing and training human resources.

Summing Up

This concludes the analyses of managerial practices utilized by American and Japanese subsidiaries and local firms in Taiwan.

Very briefly, we analyzed the managerial function of planning in Chapter 2. Chapter 3 discussed policy-making and control devices. Chapter 4 dealt with the organizational set-up. Chapter 5 examined leadership style and behavior. Lastly, this chapter analyzed manpower management practices. The managerial functions of planning, organizing, staffing, directing, motivating, and controlling have now been analyzed in some depth.

Overall, our findings indicate that American subsidiaries in Taiwan (as well as those in five other developing countries) undertake long-range planning of 5 to 10 years duration. They formulate and utilize major policies as control mechanisms and also use other control devices, such as cost and budgetary controls, quality control, etc. They tend to be somewhat decentralized in their decision-making process. While they appear to pay some degree of attention to manpower and management problems, their practices in this regard are not highly developed. In addition, these companies attempt to utilize a consultative or democratic style of leadership and manifest a certain degree of trust and confidence in their employees.

In contrast, only a few of the Japanese and local firms in Taiwan undertake long-range planning, formulate and document policies, utilize control devices, or attempt to decentralize their decision-making processes. The leadership styles in these firms can best be characterized as autocratic or paternalistic. Further, these companies have the least developed manpower management practices observed in all the companies studied.

Of course, there are a few notable exceptions among both the Japanese and local companies. These exceptional companies are quite close to the American subsidiaries in their management practices.

The reader may ask at this juncture: are advanced management practices and know-how transferable to industrial enterprises in Taiwan, or to that matter, in the other developing countries.

Our analysis is directed toward exploring this question quite deeply. Preceding this, however, it will be helpful to know something about the managerial effectiveness of the firms we investigated in Taiwan. The next chapter is developed toward this end.

CHAPTER VII

MANAGEMENT AND ENTERPRISE EFFECTIVENESS

Introduction

Previous chapters analyzed the nature of managerial practices in three sets of companies (U.S. subsidiaries, Japanese subsidiaries, and local firms) in Taiwan. In collecting and analyzing these data, there has been an implicit assumption that managerial practices contribute to managerial and enterprise effectiveness.

In making such an implicit assumption, we endorse the contention that all social organizations come into being to achieve certain objectives or goals. These goals may be specific or diffuse; but nevertheless, it is the pursuit of these goals which provide driving force to the organization.

Also inherent in this implicit assumption is the underlying functional relationship between management practices and management and enterprise effectiveness. In other words, we do not visualize management practices as an end in itself; rather, to us they are the means for achieving higher organizational effectiveness.

Purpose of this Chapter

The main purpose of this chapter is to examine management and enterprise effectiveness in the three sets of the companies studied in Taiwan. In analyzing management and enterprise effectiveness, we will examine both the behavioral and economic measures of effectiveness. Preceding this analysis, however, a brief note on the concept of effectiveness may be useful.

Concept of Effectiveness

As yet, there is no acceptable formulation of a universal conceptual scheme, methodology, or criteria for assessing organizational effectiveness.[1]

Particularly in the business and management literature, the concept of management effectiveness has been used in a varied fashion. For example, many management writers have equated management effectiveness with the economic effectiveness of an enterprise and, accordingly, suggest such measures as sales, profits, stock prices, market shares, scrap loss, and productivity.[2]

On the other hand, management and organization theorists with behavioral orientations have emphasized the measures of human resource effectiveness. These measures include such factors as employee morale, interpersonal relationships, interdepartmental relationships, and utilization of high-level manpower.

Rensis Likert, for example, has ardently argued that:

> All end-result measurements give 'after the fact' data. This is true of measurements of production, scrap, costs, earnings and all other financial data. As successful business management has demonstrated, these measurements are valuable. Nevertheless, their predictive power is limited. All too often, end result measurements can be used only to lock the barn door after the horse is stolen.[3]

In order to remedy the limitations of economic measures, Likert has suggested such behavioral measures as the level of confidence and trust among employees, motivation, loyalty, and the capacity of the organization to communicate fully, interact effectively, and arrive at sound decisions.[4]

In the same vein, many other scholars like Argyris,[5] Bennis,[6]

[1] See J. Ghorpade (ed.), *Assessment of Organizational Effectiveness* (Pacific Palisades, California: Goodyear Publishing Company, Inc., 1971), especially pp. 83-164.

[2] Jackson Martindell, *The Appraisal of Management* (New York: Harper and Row, 1962).

[3] Rensis Likert, *The Human Organization: Its Management and Value* (New York: McGraw-Hill Book Company, Inc., 1967), p. 100.

[4] *Ibid.*, p. 29.

[5] Chris Argyris, *Integrating the Individual and the Organization* (New York: John Wiley & Sons, Inc., 1964).

[6] Warren G. Bennis, *Changing Organizations: Essays on the Development and Evaluation of Human Organization* (New York: Mc-Graw-Hill Book Company, 1966).

Etzioni,[7] Georgopoulos and Tannenbaum,[8] and Selznick,[9] to mention a few, have argued for the behavioral measures to examine organizational effectiveness. These include:

1. Productivity
2. Intraorganizational stress and conflict
3. Organizational flexibility to adjust to external and internal changes
4. Interrelationships among different parts of the organization
5. Awareness of the patterns in parts of the organization
6. System effectiveness in influencing its own core activities

It is our contention that the survival and growth of a business enterprise depends not only on its financial or economic strength, but upon its utilization of human resources. Accordingly, we endeavored to collect data on both behavioral and economic measures of management and enterprise effectiveness. We were, however, more successful in gathering data on behavioral measures than those on economic measures. Many companies in Taiwan were not willing to disclose information concerning their financial affairs.

Management and Enterprise Effectiveness Measures

Specifically, data on the following factors were collected:

1. Employee morale and satisfaction in work (operative level)
2. Absenteeism
3. Employee turnover
4. Productivity
5. Ability to hire and retain high-level manpower
6. Interdepartmental relationships
7. Perception of the executive's concern of the firms's overall objectives and goals
8. Utilization of high-level manpower
9. Executive responsiveness in adapting to environmental changes
10. Overall growth and profits

[7] Amitai Etzioni, "Two Approaches to Organizational Analysis: A Critique and a Suggestion," *Administrative Science Quarterly*, V, No. 2 (September, 1960), pp. 257-258.

[8] B. S. Georgopoulos and A. S. Tannenbaum, "A Study of Organizational Effectiveness," *American Sociological Review*, Vol. 22, No. 5 (1957), pp. 534-540.

[9] Philip Selznick, "Foundations of the Theory of Organization," *American Sociological Review*, XII, No. 1 (1948), pp. 25-35.

EMPLOYEE MORALE AND SATISFACTION IN WORK (OPERATIVE LEVEL)

The concept of morale reflects the employee's attitude toward his work, group, supervisor, and company. Chester Barnard,[10] for example, has defined morale as the degree to which individual motives are gratified. In the discussion of employee morale, one comes across such words as esprit de corps, identification, satisfaction, solidarity, cohesion, and alienation.[11]

While there are contradictory findings concerning the relationship between morale and productivity, there seems to be considerable evidence overall suggesting positive relationships between these two variables.[12] Researchers have utilized various measures, such as absenteeism, turnover, employee commitment, and discipline to reflect employee morale in a given organization.

Although many researchers claim there are interrelationships between absenteeism, turnover, and employee morale, we were unable to discern such relationships in our study. This may be due to the small size of our sample and it partly reflects the impact of environmental factors on absenteeism and the turnover rate in Taiwan companies.

In this study, data on employee morale was collected by randomly interviewing selected operatives and supervisors. The sample size ranged from 12 to 20 employees in each firm. The employees were asked open-ended, non-structured questions.[13]

As shown in Table 7-1, the American subsidiaries are more successful in developing high morale among their employees than the Japanese subsidiaries and local companies. However, both of the latter companies are able to maintain average morale.

[10] Chester I. Bernard, *The Functions of Executives* (Cambridge, Mass.: Harvard University Press, 1954), pp. 56-61.

[11] See James L. Price, *Organizational Effectiveness: An Inventory of Propositions* (Homewood, Ill.: Richard D. Irwin, Inc., 1968), p. 18.

[12] See Daniel Katz, Nathan Maccoby, and Nancy C. Morse, "*Productivity, Supervision and Morale in an Office Situation* (Ann Arbor, Michigan: Survey Research Center, Institute for Social Research, 1950); and M. Argyle, G. Gardner, and F. Coffee, "Supervisory Methods Related to Productivity, Absenteeism and Labor Turnover," *Human Relations*, Vol. XI, No. 1 (1958), pp. 23-40.

[13] In the case of blue-collar employees, my research assistant, Mr. Robert Hsieh, a citizen of Taiwan, conducted these interviews in Chinese language.

Our overall view of employee morale in Taiwan is quite favorable. The Chinese worker is well-mannered, disciplined, hard-working, and reliable. This is reflected in the high productivity of the worker in Taiwan.

TABLE 7-1. *Employee Morale and Satisfaction in Work (Operative Level)*

	U.S. Subsidiary (n = 9)	Japanese Subsidiary (n = 7)	Local Firm (n = 11)
1. Excellent morale and high satisfaction in work	6	2	2
2. Average morale and somewhat satisfied in work	–	3	7
3. Poor morale and dissatisfied	2		
4. Not able to discern	1	2	2

ABSENTEEISM

In simple terms, absenteeism means a reduction in the department's efficiency, a loss for the company, and the loss of a day's pay for the employee. There is a melange of socio-economic and cultural factors which affect the rate of absenteeism. For example, one finds a greater rate of absenteeism in times of economic prosperity, rising wages, and low unemployment. Conversely, in an economic depression or recession, when jobs are scarce, absentee report forms gather dust. Yet, under a given socioeconomic and cultural environment, differences in the number of absentees among different firms might reflect their effectiveness in providing a good working atmosphere. Research studies of Argyris,[14] Fleishman and Harris,[15] Argyle, Gardner, and Coffee,[16] and Lindguist,[17] indicate a positive relationship between absenteeism, turnover, and leadership styles. To Argyris, absenteeism

[14] Argyris, *op. cit.*

[15] E. Fleishman and E. Harris, "Patterns of Leadership Behavior Related to Employee Grievances and Turnover," Department of Industrial Administration, Yale University, 1961. (Mimeographed)

[16] Argyle, Gardner and Coffee, *op. cit.*

[17] A. Lindguist, "Absenteeism and Job Turnover as Consequences of Unfavorable Job Adjustment," *Acta Social,* Vol. 3, Nos. 2 and 3 (1958), pp. 119-131.

is one kind of defensive mechanism which the employee uses to let out his frustrations, conflicts, and failures in achieving satisfaction in his work.[18] Fleishman and Harris related turnover, as well as grievance rates, to leadership behavior: "The more the leader structures, directs, and controls, the greater the probability of turnover."[19] Argyle, Gardner, and Coffee related directive leadership to absenteeism, while Lindguist demonstrated a causal relationship between unfavorable job adjustment and absenteeism.

Absenteeism in Taiwan does not seem to be a major problem. As data in Table 7-2 indicate, in the majority of American and Japanese subsidiaries absenteeism among blue-collar employees, supervisors, clerical workers, and managerial personnel is less than four per cent. The local companies, however, experience somewhat higher absenteeism among their employees.

It is interesting to note from Table 7-2 that, in the local companies,

TABLE 7-2. *Absenteeism at Various Levels*

Level		Absenteeism Rate/Year				
		25% and more	15 to 24%	5 to 14%	4% & less	Not available
U.S. Subsidiaries (n = 9)	Operative level	1		2	6	
	Supervisor	1		1	4	3
	Junior management and clerical employees		1		3	5
	Senior management				3	6
Japanese Subsidiaries (n = 7)	Operative level	1		1	5	
	Supervisor		1		3	3
	Junior management and clerical employees				3	4
	Senior management				3	4
Local Companies (n = 11)	Operative level		1	6	3	1
	Supervisor	3	5	1	1	1
	Junior management and clerical employees				5	6
	Senior management				5	6

[18] Argyris, *op. cit.*, pp. 59-60.
[19] Fleishman and Harris, *op. cit.*, quoted from Argyris, *op. cit.*, p. 60.

supervisory personnel stay away from work more frequently than operatives, clerical employees, and managerical personnel. Why is this so? Our inquiry suggests that supervisors in the local companies enjoy many privileges like sick leave, causal leave, etc. and seem to take advantage of such preferred rights. However, our interviews with the supervisors themselves indicated a high level of frustration among these "men in the middle." They have a great deal of responsibility but no decision-making power. Further, they have very few opportunities to exercise initiative in the work situation.

Overall, the absenteeism rate in Taiwan compares very favorably with other developing and developed countries. For example, absenteeism in companies in India was 12 to 15 per cent, while in the Philippines it was 12 per cent. Among American industries, 5 to 10 per cent absenteeism is considered as quite normal.

TURNOVER

The concept of labor turnover signifies an employee's decision to disengage from an organization's activities. Usually, in the management literature, labor turnover is defined as the number of people hired per unit of time in order to maintain a working force at a given figure. The most frequently used formula to measure labor turnover is: $T = R/F$, where T = turnover, R = replacements per unit of time, and F = average working force.[20]

This formula includes all kinds of labor turnover, i.e., workers leaving the organization due to death, sickness, dismissal, and for the purpose of joining other organizations.

In our study, however, we concentrated on the labor turnover that arises from the worker's decision to leave the firm in order to join another firm. Thus, in collecting data, the labor turnover due to sickness, death, and dismissal was excluded. Our data, termed here as voluntary turnover rate, may hopefully suggest a stronger relationship between employee morale and labor turnover.

Of course, voluntary labor turnover is a function of many external as well as internal factors such as: economic conditions and opportunities available; sociocultural make-up of employees; legal framework; and working conditions in the organization, including relative

[20] See E. E. Nemmers and C. C. Janzen, *Dictionary of Economics and Business* (Patterson: Littlefield Adams and Company, 1959), p. 166.

wages, opportunities for advancement, and the satisfaction derived from work. Management might not be able to control the so-called external factors influencing voluntary turnover. However, the internal factors mentioned above are in the realm of managerial influence.

Higher Turnover in Taiwan

Employee turnover seems to be the major headache for many companies in Taiwan. A sizeable number of companies experience an abnormally high rate of turnover among their blue-collar employees. This ranges from a low of 25 per cent to a high of 150 per cent of their total labor force. As can be seen from Table 7-3, more than one-third of the companies studied (11 of the 27) belong to this category. The average turnover rate in Taiwan is about 40 per cent. This is indeed very high compared to such developing countries as Argentina, Brazil, Chile, India, the Philippines, and Uruguay. The average rate of turnover in these countries is less than 10 per cent.[21]

TABLE 7-3. *Employee Turnover at Various Levels*

Level		Turnover/Year				
		25 to 150%	15 to 24%	5 to 14%	4% & less	Not available
U.S.	Operative	3		5	1	
Sub-	Supervisor	1			4	4
sidiaries	Junior management and	2		2	4	1
(n = 9)	clerical employees					
	Senior management			1	4	4
Japanese	Operative	3		1	3	
Sub-	Supervisor		1		4	2
sidiaries	Junior management and	2	1	1	3	
(n = 7)	clerical employees					
	Senior management					
Local	Operative	5	4	1	1	
Compa-	Supervisor		1	2	6	2
nies	Junior management and			5	4	2
(n = 11)	clerical employees					
	Senior management				5	6

[21] A. R. Negandhi and S. B. Prasad, *Comparative Management* (New York: Appleton-Century-Crofts, 1971), pp. 112-115.

Turnover among clerical, supervisory, and managerial personnel is not so high as among operative level employees but there, also, about one-fourth of the companies report 15 per cent or more turnover among employees at these levels.

Environmental Impact on Turnover

The high level of employee turnover in Taiwan prompted further inquiry into this problem. To this end, we held additional intensive interviews with some 50 executives, supervisors, blue-collar employees, economists, government officials, planners, and university professors. The following environmental factors were mentioned frequently in these interviews:

1. Industrial boom and shortage of skilled workers.
2. Low wages and lack of wage differentials between the industrial and non-industrial workers.

Let us examine these factors in more detail.

Industrial Boom and Shortage of Skilled Workers

As we noted earlier in Chapters 1 and 6, Taiwan has experienced phenomenal industrial growth in the last decade. For example, during 1953 to 1967, industrial production increased 14 per cent yearly. This trend continues. In the last five years, Taiwan registered a 19 per cent increase per year in the industrial sector.

It is true that, at least in the foreseeable future, Taiwan may not experience a labor shortage for the unskilled workers. But this picture is considerably different with respect to skilled employees and supervisory, managerial, and technical personnel. As already noted, many companies complained a great deal about the shortage of manpower in these categories. Executives of those companies experiencing a high level of employee turnover put greater emphasis on the labor shortage giving rise to chronic labor turnover.

Low Wages and Lack of Differential in Wages

Low wages, coupled with the high productivity of the Chinese worker, makes Taiwan a very attractive place for foreign investors. But this in itself is a mixed blessing. The lack of a reasonable wage differential between industrial and non-industrial sectors keeps some portions of the available labor force away from industry; at the same time, it also makes it easier for the industrial worker to shift jobs.

The government's martial law, which prohibits labor strikes, further aggrevates the labor turnover situation. Dissatisfied and frustrated workers, unable to bargain for improved wages and working conditions, simply quit jobs and return to the non-industrial sectors or to their own small businesses.

In the electronics industry, where turnover is a particularly serious problem, firms seek to employ girls between the ages of 16 and 19. These girls, although well-disciplined and hard-working, are not necessarily career oriented.[22]

PRODUCTIVITY AND INNOVATIVENESS

We were unable to obtain hard data on labor productivity from the many companies studied in Taiwan. Wherever this information was available, comparisons of diverse data from different industrial sectors posed another difficulty.

However, in order to gain some general perspective on the productivity of the Chinese worker, we collected the following information:

a. Scrap loss
b. Improvements made in the production process through the suggestion of employees
c. Views of American and Japanese executives about the relative productivity of the American, Japanese, and Chinese employees in their respective companies.

Scrap Loss

In a large majority of the companies, raw material wastage is less than 10 per cent. The scrap loss in finished products is also low; it varies from 5 to 15 per cent. Raw material wastage and scrap loss are largely due to the lack of storage facilities rather than the employees' "wrong doings." The Chinese worker per se is not likely to vent his frustrations by producing more wastage.

Innovativeness Of The Chinese Worker

While our inquiry into the productivity of the Chinese worker indicates a very favorable picture, our query concerning his innovative

[22] Although the productivity of female employees was high, they mainly worked to secure some money for their social life and future marriages. This was the general viewpoint of many executives in this industry.

ability suggests a more pessimistic outlook. Though well-disciplined and hard-working, the Chinese worker simply lacks innovative spirit. Of the 27 companies studied, none reports any significant improvement in either production processes or organizational matters resulting from employee suggestions.

The routine employee "suggestion box" found in many U.S. companies is non-existant in Taiwan. Moreover, American executives flatly contend that the "suggestion box" is useless in Taiwan. They all agree that change must come from the higher echelons of management. Excessive discipline, thus, does create a problem for innovations and improvements. This problem may indeed become the major bottleneck in Taiwan's future economic and industrial development. As Japan discovered, a nation cannot keep growing simply by immitation; to compete in the world markets, a country must innovate.[23]

Views on Relative Productivity

The majority of the top executives in American and Japanese subsidiaries are expatriates; accordingly, they seem to have some relative notion about employee productivity in the U.S., Japan, and Taiwan. Many of these executives also have experience in other developing countries like Hong Kong, the Philippines, and India.

During interviews with these executives, we asked this specific question: "How would you rate the productivity of the Chinese employee with other nationals you are familiar with?" In response, an overwhelming majority rated the Chinese worker as high or higher than the American, Japanese, Filipino, Indian, and the Chinese worker in Hong Kong. High employee productivity in Taiwan was also supported by specific data collected by one electronic firm manufacturing computer parts.

In summary, an inquiry into employee productivity in Taiwan suggests a very promising and optimistic outlook. However, in terms of the Chinese employee's innovative capacities, we have to report a more pessimistic outlook.

[23] M. Y. Yoshino, *Japan's Managerial System* (Cambridge: M.I.T. Press, 1968), especially Chapters 1 and 2.

MANAGEMENT EFFECTIVENESS CONCERNING HIGH-LEVEL MANPOWER

As the reader may have noted, the preceding criteria for management effectiveness dealt mainly with blue-collar employees. These are indeed important factors affecting the overall effectiveness of an organization. However, equally if not more important, are the factors concerning high-level manpower. Many behavioral theorists have equated management effectiveness with organizational effectiveness in managing high-level manpower resources.

To provide a better perspective on the managerial effectiveness of industrial enterprises in Taiwan, we also endeavored to collect data regarding the following factors:

1. Attracting and retaining high-level manpower
2. Interdepartmental relationship
3. Executive's perception of the firm's overall objectives
4. Firm's responsiveness to the changes in external environment
5. Utilization of high-level manpower

In the following section, we shall analyze these data. In order to avoid repetitive assertions, it may be pointed out here that data concerning all the factors analyzed in the following pages were collected through semi-structured interviews held with the various levels of executives and by direct observation of the company's activities.

ATTRACTING HIGH-LEVEL MANPOWER

Many economic development theorists have argued that one of the main bottlenecks in achieving rapid economic development in underdeveloped countries is the shortage of trained managerial and technical manpower.[24] As noted in the last chapter, the leaders of many developing countries have realized this and made concerted efforts to alleviate these shortages. Despite their best efforts, a shortage of trained managerial and technical personnel still persists in many of these countries, including Taiwan.

[24] Frederick Harbison and Charles A. Myers, *Management in the Industrial World: An International Analysis* (New York: McGraw-Hill Book Company, 1959), Chapter 1.

Notwithstanding the short supply of high-level manpower in Taiwan, there are considerable differences among the three sets of companies in their abilities to attract and retain trained managerial and technical personnel. For example, as shown in Table 7-4, seven of the nine U.S. subsidiaries are able to hire and retain trained managerial and technical personnel. Specifically, executives and technical personnel at the top and the middle-levels of the organizational hierarchy in these companies are college graduates. Many of these personnel earned their Master degrees from abroad, particularly in the United States. In other words, the quality of high-level manpower in the U.S. subsidiaries can be classified as "Professional."

In contrast, the Japanese subsidiaries and the local companies are unable to attract such qualified and trained personnel. The majority of the executives and technical personnel in these companies are poorly trained. For many, the main qualification for employment is their close family tie with the owner and/or the chief executive.

Why are the U.S. subsidiaries more effective than either the Japanese subsidiaries or the local companies in attracting trained personnel? Our inquiry suggests the following:

a. High monetary rewards
b. Opportunity for advancement and individual development
c. Objective criteria for promotion and rewards
d. "Gateway-entry" to enter the U.S. universities

The salary scale in U.S. subsidiaries in Taiwan (and for that matter in most underdeveloped countries) is roughly twice the prevailing scale in comparable Japanese and local companies. Invariably, U.S. subsidiaries rely on objective criteria for advancement and promotion

TABLE 7-4. *Management Effectiveness to Attract and Retain High-Level Manpower*

Management Effectiveness to Attract High-Level Manpower	U.S. Subsidiary (n = 9)	Japanese Subsidiary (n = 7)	Local Firm (n = 11)
Able to hire and retain highly trained personnel	7	1	2
Able to hire and retain average trained personnel	1	5	5
Not able to hire and retain even average trained personnel	1	1	4

whereby the road to the top (except perhaps at the managing director level) is open to all those who are able to demonstrate the competence required for specific positions in the organization. In other words, individuals are not held down because of their low social and family status or their lack of blood relationships with the bosses. In many of the Japanese subsidiaries and local companies in Taiwan, such criteria do play an important role.

For many young college graduates in Taiwan, the U.S. companies also represent a "gateway" for fulfilling higher aspirations which include further graduate training in U.S. universities. Unfortunately, the majority of those who succeed in entering U.S. universities never return, therefore, only adding to the already existing "brainrain" in Taiwan.

Environmental Factors Affecting Professionalization of Managers

In recent years, scholars have paid considerable attention to the problems of high-level manpower resources in developing countries. Among others, we cite the pioneering studies of Harbison and Myers and their collaborators.[25] These authors revealed that the lack of proper governmental and business planning has been responsible for the dearth of educational institutions needed to train managers in these countries.

Other authors have underscored the importance of social and cultural variables affecting the professionalization of managers. The socio-cultural factors identified by various authors are:[26]

1. Society's views toward business and business leaders
2. Government's views toward business and business leaders
3. Religious beliefs and practices
4. Class structures and status symbols
5. Importance attached to the family ties
6. Bureaucratization of society at large, and the government in particular.[27]

[25] *Ibid.*, also see by the same authors *Education, Manpower and Economic Growth* (New York: McGraw-Hill Book Company, Inc., 1964).

[26] See R. N. Farmer and B. M. Richman, *Comparative Management and Economic Progress* (Homewood, Ill.: Richard D. Irwin, Inc., 1965); and UNESCO, *Report on the World Situation* (Paris, March 9, 1961).

[27] C. K. Yang, "Some Characteristics of Chinese Bureaucratic Behavior," *The Confucianism in Action*, ed. by D. S. Nivison and A. F. Wright (Palo Alto: Stanford University Press), p. 150.

Although we do not deny the impact of these socio-cultural factors on the professionalization of managers, our observations in Taiwan suggest that the owner-manager situation and the prevailing market conditions have had considerable affect on the professional level attained by these managers. Let us examine these factors in more detail.

As in most other developing nations, many of Taiwan's industrial enterprises are owned and managed by members of a family. Family ownership tends to deter the emergence of professional managers. There is no "room at the top" for "outsiders," regardless of training. In other words, as Fillol has observed in the case of Argentina, "when the road upward is blocked by family barriers ... people may look at their job as a mere foothold from which to launch their own business careers."[28]

Seller's Market Conditions

As noted before, many industrial enterprises in Taiwan operate in sheltered market conditions where the demand for many products overruns the corresponding supply of goods. The seller's market condition assures handsome profits to the firm regardless of its cost structure or product quality. Under such market conditions, many of the firms in Taiwan feel that expenditures to employ and develop professional managers are unnecessary "expenses" and should be avoided.

INTERDEPARTMENTAL RELATIONS

This effectiveness criterion refers to the degree of interdependence among the various sub-units (departments) within an organization. Specifically, information was sought concerning how well each department recognized its interdependence with other departments, and how well the various departments got along with each other.[29] In collecting and evaluating data on this factor, we relied heavily on what we observed rather than what we were told by the executives themselves. For the purpose of comparison and analysis, our overall observations in each firm were categorized in the following manner:

[28] Tomás Roberto Fillol, *Social Factors in Economic Development: The Argentine Case* (Cambridge, Mass.: The M.I.T. Press, 1963), p. 61.

[29] For importance of this criterion see Argyris, *op. cit.*, p. 174.

a. Very cooperative
b. Somewhat cooperative
c. Hardly cooperative

As can be seen from Table 7-5, the U.S. subsidiaries are able to achieve higher cooperation among the various units or departments. Specifically, in six of the nine U.S. subsidiaries interdepartmental relations are very cooperative; in two subsidiaries the relations among units are somewhat cooperative. Such relations are poor in only one U.S. subsidiary. In contrast, the majority of the Japanese subsidiaries and local companies reflect interdepartmental relations which are neither cooperative nor poor; they are somewhat cooperative.

Why are the U.S. subsidiaries able to achieve higher interdepartmental cooperation? Our inquiry reveals that, in the U.S. companies, clear statements of objectives, goals, and procedures for each department and for the organization as a whole contribute greatly toward this end. Also, many executives interviewed mentioned the role played by impartial and objective appraisal systems and objective promotion and reward criteria.

Executives in the Japanese subsidiaries and local firms, on the contrary, show much jealousy and rivalry. In these companies, there is also an apparent lack of specifically stated objectives, goals, and procedures.

TABLE 7-5. *Cooperation among Units or Departments*

Interdepartmental Relationship	U.S. Subsidiary (n = 9)	Japanese Subsidiary (n = 7)	Local Firm (n = 11)
Very cooperative	6	2	2
Somewhat cooperative	2	3	7
Hardly cooperative	1	2	2

THE EXECUTIVE'S PERCEPTION OF THE FIRM'S OVERALL OBJECTIVES

This variable deals with the question of how a firm's overall objectives and the achievement of those objectives are perceived by influential participants in the organization. The term perception is not used in a strict sense, but rather to connote the executive's "point of view."

Indeed, this factor is closely related to, but not identical to, our criterion of "interdependence of different parts" discussed above. Whereas the latter deals with the so-called working relationships between different parts of the organization, the former factor sheds light on how the participants themselves view the organizational objectives and their roles in achieving them.

Both of these measures, interdependence of different parts and the executive's perception of achieving the firm's overall objectives, were fashioned after Argyris's "Mix Model" variables. The importance of the criterion for achieving the firm's overall objectives is explained by Argyris in these terms:

> An organization as a whole has, by definition, objectives that it must achieve. To be sure, every part has formal sub-objectives, but these take on their meanings by being related to the larger overall objectives. The less an organization is guided by its overall objectives and the more the objectives of each part become paramount and are not relatable to the overall objectives, the less the firm approximates the essential characteristics of organization.[30]

Data concerning this measure were collected by asking top- and middle-level executives of different departments about the objectives of the firm as they perceived them.

In other words, indirect questioning was directed toward ascertaining the awareness of the executive concerning the overall objectives of the firm. The executives were also asked whether they placed more emphasis on achieving the firm's overall objectives or the objectives of their departments. On the basis of this information, we categorized each firm as follows:

a. Systems optimization was perceived as most important
b. Sub-systems optimization was perceived as equally important
c. Sub-systems optimization was perceived as the ultimate goal

As the data presented in Table 7-6 show, executives of the American subsidiaries view achieving of the firm's overall objectives as most crucial. Specifically, such an impression was gained from seven of the nine U.S. subsidiaries. In contrast, only three of the seven Japanese subsidiaries and three of the eleven local companies are able to emphasize the achievement of the firm's overall objectives as most important. In other words, in the latter companies, departmental goals preoccupy the executives' time and talent.

[30] *Ibid.*, p. 153.

As to the reasons why American subsidiaries are successful in emphasizing the firm's overall objectives while Japanese subsidiaries and local firms are not, our findings indicate that clearer statements of goals, objectives, procedures, and practices to achieve these goals contribute a geat deal. A lack of clarity or fuzziness concerning the firm's overall goals and objectives tends to distort the executives' perception of the firm's overall objectives and goals. Excessive rigidity in the procedures and practices to achieve stated goals, as well as strict adherence to the stated goals, also may lead to frustration and anxiety. We also observed this situation in two American subsidiaries and one Japanese subsidiary.

TABLE 7-6. *Executive's Perceptions of the Firm's Overall Objectives*

	U.S. Subsidiary (n = 9)	Japanese Subsidiary (n = 7)	Local Firm (n = 11)
Systems optimization was perceived as the most important	7	3	3
Sub-systems optimization was perceived as equally important	1	2	4
Sub-systems optimization was perceived as the ultimate goal	1	2	4

UTILIZATION OF HIGH-LEVEL MANPOWER

To collect data on this aspect, we made inquiries at two levels: (1) How the executives spent their working time; and (2) how zealous they were in their work. These data are concerned only with top-level executives (e.g. president, general manager, sales manager, production manager, etc.).

Although the executive's job involves a variety of tasks, it seems to be a consensus among management writers that the important functions of an executive are policy-making, long-range planning, and coordination of various departmental activities. Of course, the relative importance assigned to various executive functions depends on the structure and nature of the industry, the competition, and the socio-economic, political, and legal conditions prevailing during a particular period. For example, in a country, or in a specific industry for that matter, where governmental controls and bureaucracy are excessive, senior executives may be required to spend their time dealing with governmental officials. In other cases, where labor problems are most acute, senior executives may need to spend considerable time resolving labor problems.

Since our data were collected from companies facing similar socio-economic, political, and legal conditions in Taiwan, these comparative data may provide some perspective on how well the companies utilize their high-level manpower.

As data in Table 7-7 indicate, American subsidiaries seem to emphasize policy-making, long-range planning, and co-ordination as major functions for their senior executives. Such emphasis is also found in one Japanese subsidiary and four local companies. Thus, American subsidiaries are most careful in utilizing their high-level manpower, while the Japanese are the least careful. Local companies score in between these two extremes. However, in terms of executive enthusiasm and drive, Japanese subsidiaries appear to be as successful as the

TABLE 7-7. *Utilization of High-Level Manpower*

Utilization of High-Level Manpower	U.S. Subsidiary (n = 9)	Japanese Subsidiary (n = 7)	Local Firm (n = 11)
A. How Executives Spend Their Time			
1. Policy-making and long-range planning	3	1	2
2. Coordination with other departments	3		2
3. Routine work and finding faults with subordinates	3	6	7
B. Executives' Enthusiasm and Drive			
1. Enormous drive and enthusiasm	5		3
2. Moderate drive and enthusiams	2	4	3
3. Withdrawing and defensive individuals	2	3	5

local companies in aspiring their high-level manpower. Of course, American subsidiaries are more effective than either the Japanese or local companies in this area. Only in two of the nine U.S. subsidiaries were we able to discern withdrawing and defensive individuals at the senior executive level. By contrast, we found such individuals in roughly half of the Japanese and local companies.

EXECUTIVE RESPONSIVENESS IN ADAPTING TO ENVIRONMENTAL CHANGES

This factor pertains to a firm's capacity to adapt to environmental changes. To collect data, we observed the executive's calmness in responding to environmental changes affecting his firm. To an extent, a firm's ability to cope with environmental changes depends upon how well it has been able to control its own internal workings of the organization, as well as its responsiveness to external forces.

Because of the foreign origin of the American subsidiaries, one would expect that these companies would have the most difficult time in understanding and adapting to Taiwan's environmental conditions. One could likewise expect, then, that local companies and Japanese subsidiaries might find it relatively easier to cope with environmental changes. However, our observation in these firms reveals a different picture. American subsidiaries seem to have adapted well to Taiwan's environmental conditions and their executives are well prepared for

TABLE 7-8. *The Executives' Responsiveness in Adapting to Environmental Changes*

	U.S. Subsidiary (n = 9)	Japanese Subsidiary (n = 7)	Local Firm (n = 11)
Executive's Responsiveness in Adapting to Environmental Conditions			
Able to adapt without much difficulty	4	1	3
Able to adapt with some difficulty	4	6	3
Able to adapt with considerable difficulty	1	0	5

environmental changes. Strangely enough, executives in the local companies complained the most and seemed the least able to adapt to changes in the environment. Executives in the Japanese subsidiaries seem able to adapt to environmental changes but not without some difficulty. (See Table 7-8.)

Our research in Argentina, Brazil, India, the Philippines, and Uruguay indicates similar patterns. That is, American subsidiaries in those countries have less difficulty in adapting to environmental changes than their counterpart local firms.

Enterprise Effectiveness

In order to evaluate enterprise effectiveness, we endeavored to collect data on the following factors:

1. Return on sales and on investment
2. Growth in market share
3. Increase in sales in the last five years
4. Growth in price of stock and P/E ratios
5. Unit costs
6. Utilization of plant facilities

Unfortunately, comparable and reliable data on these items were not available from many of the companies studied. This was partly due to poor record-keeping practices in the local companies and partly due to an unwillingness to reveal such information in all three sets of companies. Faced with this situation, we decided to evaluate the firms' overall growth in sales and profits. The information was obtained by talking with employees at various levels (e.g., manager, supervisor, technical personnel, accountant, etc.). The data collected thus reveals that the American subsidiaries have experienced growth in sales ranging from two- to ten-fold in the last five years (1963-1968). The growth in profits for these companies ranged from 25 per cent to 100 per cent of their total investment.

The Japanese subsidiaries and local companies experienced growth in sales and profits also, but at much lower rates. Sales growth in these companies ranged from zero per cent to 200 per cent in the last five years, while profits ranged from 10 per cent to 50 per cent.

Summary

This chapter analyzed management and enterprise effectiveness in U.S. subsidiaries, Japanese subsidiaries, and the local companies in

Taiwan. A total of ten factors of effectiveness were evaluated. These criteria included both behavioral and economic measures of effectiveness. Specific criteria analyzed were: employee morale, absenteeism, turnover, productivity, ability to hire and retain high-level manpower, interdepartmental relationships, executive perception of the firm's overall objectives and goals, utilization of high-level manpower, executive responsiveness in adapting to environmental changes, and the firm's overall growth in sales and profits.

Overall, U.S. subsidiaries are more effective than both the Japanese subsidiaries and the local firms. More specifically, U.S. subsidiaries are able to attain higher employee morale and productivity and lower absenteeism. They are also able to attract highly trained managerial and technical personnel. They achieve cooperation in interdepartmental relationships and effectively utilize their high-level manpower. They also experience higher growth in sales and profits than do the other two groups of firms.

Although the Japanese subsidiaries and local firms are able to maintain at least average employee morale, low absenteeism, and high productivity, these firms are less effective in attracting high-level manpower.

Both the U.S. subsidiaries and the local companies, however, experience a high rate of turnover among their employees. Only the Japanese firms seem able to maintain a low-level turnover. Environmental factors seem to have the greatest impact on turnover in Taiwan.

CHAPTER VIII

SUMMARY AND CONCLUSIONS MANAGEMENT TRANSFER: FEASIBILITY AND USEFULNESS

Introduction

We have now completed our background analyses of data concerning management practices and effectiveness in the U.S. subsidiaries, Japanese subsidiaries, and the local firms in Taiwan.

To recall, these data were collected from 27 firms (9 U.S. subsidiaries, 7 Japanese subsidiaries, and 11 local companies) through personal interviews. A structured interview guide was utilized to collect necessary information. Besides using interviews, we also conducted a questionnaire survey among 300 industrial firms in Taiwan, 99 of which filled out and returned the questionnaire (76 local firms and 23 U.S. subsidiaries).

Other details on the research design and method, as well as the rationale of comparing U.S. subsidiaries, Japanese subsidiaries, and local firms, have been given in Chapter 1 and Appendices A and B.

As stated in Chapter 1, the main purpose of our research in Taiwan and other developing countries was to examine the feasibility and usefulness of transferring advanced management practices and know-how from industrially developed countries to the developing nations. The need for management transfer processes is based on the assumption that managerial input plays a crucial role in the industrialization and economic development of underdeveloped countries. In other words, we suspect that the real bottleneck in economic and industrial development process is not a lack of knowledge concerning planning and resource allocation, but rather it is the "managerial" aspect of the developing process. This has been recognized increasingly in the last few years. For example, Si-Chin Kao, General Manager of the China Productivity and Trade Center, has stated his concern in these words:

> ... the future development must depend upon a modernized and systematic education ... while modern Western management principles and techniques should be adopted and adapted carefully ... business and industry in the Republic of China must be managed along modern lines. The old-fashioned favoritism, paternalism, and family-centered management must give way to the cold-blooded modern objective and scientific management.[1]

Purpose of this Chapter

In this final chapter, therefore, we will attempt to discern the feasibility and utility of management transfer on the basis of data collected from the three sets of industrial firms in Taiwan. In so doing we shall first define the notions of "Management Transfer" and "Advanced Management Practices and Know-How," then review briefly the nature of management practices and effectiveness observed in our Taiwan research. Finally, in order to examine the usefulness of advanced management practices and know-how, we shall explore the nature of the relationships between management practices and management effectiveness.

Definition of Advanced Management Practices

Although many authors have advocated the transfer of advanced management practices, skills, and know-how from developed countries to developing countries, few have defined the concept of "advanced management" itself.

For the purpose of this study, we adopted the definition of advanced management provided by the AIESEC International. It is defined as "the special capabilities that make a manager what he is: The capacity to collect, process, and evaluate information; the ability to distinguish the alternatives and make decisions; and the resourcefulness in communicating to others the reasons behind his decisions and actions."[2]

Translated into operational terms, this may involve the following:

1. Systematic and detailed long-range planning of goals and a means of reaching these goals.

[1] Si-chin Kao, "Modern Management Development in Taiwan Today," *Industry of Free China* (February, 1969), p. 8.

[2] "International Transfer of Management Skills," *AIESEC International News Letter* (February, 1968), p. 1.

2. Greater involvement of member participants in decision-making, both in the planning process and general organizational activities.
3. Objective measurements of the achievements against targeted goals.
4. Explanation of deviations between the achievements and targeted goals.
5. Exercising the leadership that will contribute most in increasing employee satisfaction in work and productivity.
6. Establishing selection, training, and promotion procedures which will be more conducive to higher productivity.
7. Soliciting employee cooperation, at all levels, in achieving the firm's objectives or goals.
8. Utilization of techniques and methods, such as cost accounting, quality control, and budgeting, which will enable the firm to reduce cost.

Concept of Management Transfer

As Phillip Perera has pointed out, management transfer involves three interrelated elements: (a) management knowledge; (b) management skills; and (c) management attitudes.[3]

Management knowledge refers to the tools and techniques concerning the management of productive enterprises (e.g., operation research, quality control, cost accounting and budgeting, etc.).

Management skills involve the managerial ability to implement and effectively use management tools and techniques.

Management attitudes refer to the points of view or perception of managers concerning managerial tasks, human beings, and environmental settings.

To put it differently, as Gennaro[4] has argued, the international transfer of management knowledge and skills involves three sub-sets of the problem. One is concerned with the transmission of information, the second is the learning process, and the third is the transfer process.

The transmission of information itself involves three aspects – technical, semantic, and effectiveness. The technical aspect concerns the accuracy with which symbols of communications can be transmitted. The semantic aspect refers to the precision with which the transmitted symbols convey desired meanings, and the effectiveness aspect deals

[3] Phillip Perera, "Government to Government Assistance: The International Transfer of Management Skills," *The Quarterly Journal of AIESEC International*, Vol. IV, No. 3 (August-October, 1968), p. 31.

[4] E. de Gennaro, "International Transfer of Management Skills: The Behavioral Patterns, A Preliminary Study," *The Quarterly Journal of AIESEC International*, Vol. V, No. 1 (January-March, 1969), pp. 39-48.

with the issue of how received meanings effect behavior in the "desired" manner.

The learning process involves the acquisition of technical and managerial skills and attitude formation.

The transfer process refers to the application of the knowledge received and learned in a way which will lead to effective behavior consistent with given environmental-cum-cultural settings.

To sum up, the above discussion suggests that the international transfer of management practices, know-how, and techniques involves not only the transmission of information (knowledge) concerning advanced managerial practices, know-how, and techniques, but, in its implication, also necessitates the changes and formulation of new managerial attitudes.

Obviously, the transmission of knowledge is perhaps the easiest component of the management transfer process, while the attitudinal changes may be the most difficult task. Let us now examine the types of approaches suggested thus far to accomplish this goal.

Main Focuses to Examine and Affect Management Transfer

In comparative management literature, one can discern two main focuses through which the management transfer process can be studied and undertaken. These are through the study of (a) transfer agents, such as multinational firms, business schools, international technical programs, etc; and (b) the environmental context in a given country in which management transfer is to be undertaken.

Briefly, studies of transfer agents are useful, but they suffer mainly from the methodological problem of comparability of contextual situations (e.g., sample size, technological and capital resources of the firm, etc.).

Similarly, studies of the environment and cultural context of a given country may provide useful insights for introducing advanced management practices. But the usefulness of such studies is severely limited because of the extreme difficulty in establishing causal relationships between environmental factors and management practices and effectiveness.[5]

[5] For a detailed discussion of environmental impact on management practices, see A. R. Negandhi and S. B. Prasad, *Comparative Management* (New York: Appleton-Century-Crofts, 1971), pp. 12-15.

Approach of this Study

The approach utilized in this study, as well as in the larger study undertaken in Argentina, Brazil, Chile, Greece, India, the Philippines, and Uruguay, consisted of studying the management practices and effectiveness of U.S. subsidiaries and comparable local firms in each country. The rationale of this approach rests on the contention that the American subsidiaries in foreign countries are more progressive in their management practices and have been able to achieve higher effectiveness by the advanced nature of their management practices. They are also in the advantageous position of learning the best possible management practices from their parent companies in the United States.

The examination of management practices and effectiveness of U.S. subsidiaries in a given country will thus reveal the feasibility and limitations of the transfer of advanced management practices in given environmental-cum-cultural settings. An examination of management practices and effectiveness in the comparable local firms, on the other hand, will suggest the actual differences between *what is feasible, and what is not being done but could be done.*

In our study in Taiwan, we also included the Japanese subsidiaries in our sample to examine whether the adaptive processes undergone by these firms were a relevant and worthwhile experience for the local firms in Taiwan.

If we accept the notion that the transfer of advanced management practices, know-how, and techniques requires both the transmission of knowledge and appropriate changes in managerial attitudes, then our research approach seems to be at least useful in ascertaining the types of advanced management practices, know-how, and techniques utilized by the three sets of companies located in Taiwan. In other words, by documenting the managerial practices of these companies we should be able to indicate the feasibility of utilizing certain practices and techniques. (Bear in mind, of course, these data will not enbable us to infer how such practices were learned and acquired.) Next, by exploring the relationships between management practices and management effectiveness, we should be in a position to inquire about the utility aspect of advanced management practices.

Although attitudinal changes and the formation of new managerial attitudes were beyond the scope of this study, we were able to collect preliminary data on existing managerial attitudes on many aspects of managerial tasks (through the questionnaire survey). Analyses of these data revealed some interesting changes going on in Taiwan.

Despite the many limitations of our approach, the real question is: "What did we learn from this exercise?" In the following pages we shall attempt to outline our experience in this regard. Let us begin by drawing up profiles of the overall management practices and effectiveness of the U.S. subsidiaries, the Japanese subsidiaries, and the local firms in Taiwan.

A profile of management practices and effectiveness will include a firm's orientation toward planning, policy-making, control devices, organizational set-up, the degree of decentralization, leadership style, manpower management practices, and management effectiveness in handling its human resources.

The overall profiles of management practices and effectiveness in the U.S. subsidiaries, the Japanese subsidiaries, and the local firms are outlined in Table 8-1. A word of caution is necessary in interpreting these profiles since they represent only the typical firm in each category. There were, of course, considerable differences among the firms in each set of companies.

TABLE 8-1. *Profiles of Management Practices and Effectiveness of the U.S. Subsidiary, Japanese Subsidiary, and the Local Firm*

Management Practices and Effectiveness	U.S. Subsidiary	Japanese Subsidiary	Local Firm
Planning	Long range (5 to 10 years)	Medium to short range (1 to 2 years)	Medium to short range (1 to 2 years)
Policy-making	Formally stated, utilized as guidelines and control measures	Formally not stated. Not utilized as guidelines and control measures	Formally not stated. Not utilized as guidelines and control measures
Other Control Devices Used	Quality control, cost and budgetary control. Maintenance. Setting of standards	Quality control Maintenance	Some cost control Some quality control. Some maintenance

TABLE 8-1 (*continued*)

Management Practices and Effectiveness	U.S. Subsidiary	Japanese Subsidiary	Local Firm
Organizational Set-up			
Grouping of activities	On functional-area basis	On functional-area basis	On functional-area basis
Number of departments	5 to 7	5 to 7	5 to 7
Use of specialized staff	Some	None	None
Use of service department	Considerable	Some	Some
Authority definition	Clear	Unclear	Unclear
Degree of Decentralization	High	Low	Low
Leadership			
Style	Consultative	Autocratic	Paternalistic-autocratic
Trust and confidence in subordinates	High	Low	Low
Managers' attitudes toward leadership style and delegation	Would prefer autocratic style. Authority should be held tight at the top	Not available	Would prefer consultative type
Manpower Management Practices			
Manpower policies	Formally stated	Not stated	Not stated
Organization of Personnel Dept.	Not separate unit	Not separate unit	Not separate unit
Job evaluation	Done	Done	Done by very few
Development of selection and promotion criteria	Formally done	Done by some	Done by some
Training programs	Only for the blue-collar employees	Only for the blue-collar employees	Only for the blue-collar employees
Compensation and motivation	Monetary only	Monetary only	Monetary only

TABLE 8-1 (*continued*)

Management Practices and Effectiveness	U.S. Subsidiary	Japanese Subsidiary	Local Firm
Management Effectiveness			
Employee morale	High	Moderate	Moderate
Absenteeism	Low	Low	Low
Turnover	High	Low	High
Productivity	High	High	High
Ability to attract trained personnel	Able to do so	Somewhat able to do so	Somewhat able to do so
Interdepartmental relationships	Very cooperative	Somewhat cooperative	Somewhat cooperative
Executives' perception of the firm's overall objectives	Systems optimization as an important goal	Sub-systems optimization as an important goal	Sub-systems optimization as an important goal
Utilization of high-level manpower	Effectively utilized	Moderate to poor utilization	Moderate to poor utilization
Adapting to environmental changes	Able to adapt without much difficulty	Able to adapt with some difficulty	Able to adapt with considerable difficulty
Growth in sales	Phenomenal	Considerable	Considerable to modest

PROFILES OF MANAGEMENT PRACTICES AND EFFECTIVENESS

U.S. Subsidiary

Long-range planning of 5 to 10 years' duration seems to be the common practice of U.S. subsidiaries in Taiwan, as well as in other developing countries. The typical U.S. subsidiary also formulates its long-range plans in detail and involves all levels of managerial, technical, and supervisory personnel in the planning process. *The policy making* task is taken quite seriously by this type of firm. Efforts are made to use major policies effectively, both as guidelines and as instruments of overall control to achieve the firm's objectives. Major policies are made by top level executives but, in their formulation, all levels of managerial and technical personnel are consulted and their views considered. These policies are generally concentrated in the areas of pricing, personnel selection, plant-investment, and salary and wage standards.

However, employee training, employee relations, purchasing, acquisition, and expansion receive much less emphasis. This is also true of the typical Japanese subsidiary and the typical local firm in Taiwan. *Other control devices* used by the U.S. subsidiary include cost and budgetary controls, quality control, the maintenace of equipment, and settings of work standards for the blue-collar, supervisory, clerical, and managerial personnel. Such techniques as time and motion study and periodic management audit systems, however, are not used by this or any other firm in Taiwan.

The organization setup is somewhat different in the U.S. subsidiary in Taiwan as compared to the U.S. parent company. The subsidiary is organized on the basis of major business functions (e.g., production, sales, accounting, and finance). However, the personnel function does not receive much emphasis. The typical firm has five to seven departments. Specialized staff personnel are not found frequently. Service and maintenance departments are well organized.

Authority definition is clear for each position in the organization. The degree of decentralization in decision-making is geater in the U.S. subsidiary than in the typical Japanese subsidiary and local firm. Attitudes of the U.S. subsidiary's executives regarding decentralization are only partially consistent with their practices.

The leadership style used in the U.S. subsidiary can best be characterized as democratic or consultative. Executives in the U.S. subsidiary manifest a great deal of trust and confidence in their subordinates. However, attitudes of the executives in the U.S. subsidiary are not totally consistent with their leadership styles.

Manpower management practices are the least developed areas in all the companies in Taiwan. The personnel department is not organized as a separate unit, nor is a specialized, trained personnel manager employed. The U.S. subsidiary, however, indicates some sophistication in a few of the manpower management practices. Specifically, manpower management policies are formally stated and such personnel techniques as job evaluation, development of selection and promotion criteria for managerial and technical personnel, and training programs for the blue-collar employees are utilized by the U.S. subsidiary. However, there is not much sophistication in the compensation and motivational techniques and practices utilized by this type of firm.

Managerial effectiveness, in terms of handling human resources, was found to be "excellent" in some aspects and "poor" in others. For example, the typical U.S. subsidiary does not find it difficult to attain high employee morale and productivity. However, it experiences a great deal of employee turnover. Environmental factors seem to play an important part here. On the other hand, absenteeism is not a major problem. Employee productivity is high and scrap loss is very low.

With regard to high-level manpower, the U.S. subsidiary is able to attract and retain trained managerial and technical personnel, achieve cooperative departmental relationships, and effectively utilize high-level manpower. It is also able to adopt and respond to environmental changes without much difficulty. By and large, the U.S. subsidiary makes good profits and is expanding its sales considerably.

Japanese Subsidiary

The planning orientation of the Japanese subsidiary can best be characterized as medium to short-range. The typical firm in this category plans for a one- to two-year period, although the resulting plans are less comprehensive and detailed. Review procedures, as well as strict adherence to the planned targets, are taken less seriously than in the U.S. subsidiary. There is relatively less participation of other echelons of managers in the planning activities.

Policy making is less formalized and generally not documented. No serious attempts are made to utilize major policies as guidelines or control mechanisms; however, some other forms of *control devices* are utilized. These include quality control, cost control, and maintenance of equipment.

The *organizational setup* in this type of firm is not very different from that of the U.S. subsidiary. For example, the various divisions and departments within the firm are organized on the basis of such major business functions as production, sales, purchasing, etc. Similar to the U.S. subsidiary and the local firm, the typical Japanese subsidiary has five to seven departments. However, the departmental lines are not clear-cut. The firm does not utilize specialized staff personnel, although a service department is utilized to some extent.

Authority definition is very unclear and diffuse. The degree of decentralization is low when compared to the U.S. subsidiary, but nearly the same compared to the local firm. The *leadership style* is best characterized as autocratic; trust and confidence in subordinates is low.

Manpower management practices are those least developed. The personnel department itself is not organized as a separate unit, nor is a qualified, trained personnel manager employed. No attempts have been made to formulate manpower policies.

Job-evaluation techniques, however, are utilized in some form or another. Some attempts are also made to formulate selection and promotion criteria. *Training and development* programs are poor and used for blue-collar employees only. Compensation and motivational techniques being utilized are simple and mainly monetary in nature.

The management effectiveness in a typical Japanese subsidiary is about average compared to the U.S. subsidiary. For example, employee morale in this firm is moderate; absenteeism is low; turnover is low; and productivity is high. The Japanese subsidiaries in general are the only companies in Taiwan experiencing lower turnover among their employees.

In terms of high-level manpower, the Japanese subsidiary is less successful in attracting and retaining trained managerial and technical personnel. Interdepartmental relationships among different departments are somewhat cooperative and the managers in this firm seem to stress sub-optimization of the company's overall goals and objectives. Also, this firm is not effectively utilizing its high-level manpower and is experiencing some difficulties in adapting to environmental changes. Growth in sales and profits, however, are considerable in this type of firm.

The Local Firm

The planning orientation of the local firm is medium to short-range. The resulting plans are less comprehensive and detailed and the review procedure is relatively poor. There is not much participation in the planning processes.

The policy-making task is undertaken on an ad-hoc basis. Generally, the major and functional policies are not spelled out and documented and little effort is made to utilize policies either as guidelines or as control mechanisms. Concerning lower level managers, there is relatively less participation in policy formulation. If the policies are formulated at all, the top executive or the owner himself undertakes this task.

The organizational setup is not much different from that of the typical U.S. and Japanese subsidiaries. Departments and divisions are organized on a functional basis with five to seven departments in the typical local firm. No specialized staff personnel are utilized, but a service department is used frequently.

Authority definition is unclear and diffuse. There are many instances of authority overlaps and the degree of decentralization is low. In other words, the firm is highly centralized in its decision-making. Managerial attitudes on the delegation of authority are consistent with actual practices.

Leadership style can best be characterized as paternalistic-autocratic. Trust and confidence in subordinates is low. Managerial attitudes concerning the leadership role appear to be inconsistent and ambivalent with what managers actually practice. There is some desire on the part of the managers for a democratic style of leadership.

Manpower management practices are those least developed. The personnel department is not organized as a separate unit. There are no qualified and trained personnel to undertake activities relating to human resources. Manpower policies are not formally stated and documented.

Job evaluation is infrequent and done only in a few instances. Only a few firms have developed selection and promotion criteria. Much emphasis is placed on age and experience for selecting and promoting personnel at managerial and supervisory levels.

Training programs are not well developed and emphasize only on-the-job training for operatives. Those compensation and motivational devices used are based on monetary rewards.

Management effectiveness is low compared to the U.S. subsidiary. For example, employee morale is moderate and turnover high. Nevertheless, this firm somehow manages to obtain high productivity and low levels of absenteeism in its work force. In terms of high-level manpower, the local firm is comparable to the Japanese subsidiary. It is able to hire and retain average trained managerial and technical personnel. The interdepartmental relationships are somewhat cooperative, although various managers emphasize departmental goals rather than overall firm goals as their main objectives. The local firm, by and large, is unable to effectively utilize its high-level manpower and has considerable difficulty in adapting to environmental changes. Growth in sales and profits in this firm is modest.

SUMMING UP

This brief description of management practices and effectiveness profiles in three sets of firms in Taiwan seems to reveal the following patterns:

American subsidiaries, by and large, are able to undertake long-range planning, formulate and utilize major policies as guidelines and control mechanisms, utilize other control devices, such as cost and budgetary controls, and quality controls. They likewise provide controls and delegate authority to subordinates, decentralize decision making, and allow a consultative type of leadership to be practiced. Further, they at least partially utilize some manpower management techniques, such as job evaluation.

In terms of managerial effectiveness, U.S. subsidiaries achieve high employee morale and productivity and, although they suffer a high turnover rate, they experience low absenteeism among their employees. They are successful in achieving higher effectiveness in terms of high-level manpower. Sales and growth rates also are relatively higher.

In contrast, only a few of the Japanese subsidiaries and local firms undertake long-range planning or formulate and utilize major policies as guidelines and control devices. Only a few have decentralized decision-making. Leadership styles in these firms remain either autocratic or paternalistic. Executives of these companies are unwilling to delegate authority to their subordinates. Manpower management practices in these companies are mostly underdeveloped.

Employee morale in these firms is moderate, but productivity is high and absenteeism low. However, employee turnover in the local companies is abnormally high, while it is lowest in the Japanese subsidiaries.

The effectiveness of these firms in handling high-level manpower is on the low side. Sales and growth rates are moderate.

The Big Question: Is Management Transfer Feasible?

This then brings up the important question: IS IT FEASIBLE TO TRANSFER ADVANCED MANAGEMENT PRACTICES INTO INDUSTRIAL ENTERPRISES IN TAIWAN?

On the basis of our findings, the answer to this question is affirmative for the U.S. subsidiaries. With respect to both the Japanese subsidiaries and the local firms, the answer is less assertive. Some of the

Japanese and the local companies have introduced advanced management practices, while others have not. It would be difficult, indeed, to fully explain why some of these companies do not introduce advanced management practices. We do not know for certain whether their failure to introduce advanced management practices results from inability or an unwillingness to do so.

Many cross-cultural management researchers have advanced the thesis that socio-cultural factors are the real obstacles in introducing advanced management practices and know-how into industrial enterprises in developing countries.[6] Of course, it would be naive to argue that societal environments do not affect management practices and effectiveness. However, our findings suggest that the present emphasis on the cultural explanation is somewhat exaggerated.

Our research findings in Taiwan, particularly, as well as in other developing countries, compel us to adopt cautious attitudes in this regard.[7] Although this study reveals that socio-economic and cultural factors have considerable impact on labor turnover, various elements of management practices and effectiveness seem to be under the overall purview of managerial control.

Our data on managerial attitudes (obtained through the questionnaire survey) toward many aspects of managerial tasks also fails to reveal subtle differences among the American and the Chinese executives.

THE OTHER BIG QUESTION: IS IT USEFUL?

Without entering into endless dialogue concerning the socio-cultural impact on management practices, we need to explore one other big question: IS IT USEFUL TO TRANSFER ADVANCED MANAGEMENT PRACTICES AND KNOW-HOW INTO INDUSTRIAL ENTERPRISES IN DEVELOPING COUNTRIES?

The answer to this question is vital if we are to make a rational decision whether to introduce advanced management practices into these countries. In other words, if the answer is "no," then one need not even bother to question the feasibility of introducing such practices into developing countries.

[6] See Richard N. Farmer and Barry M. Richman, *Comparative Management and Economic Progress* (Homewood: Richard D. Irwin, 1965).

[7] Negandhi and Prasad, *op. cit.*

In order to provide a systematic answer to this question, we made some attempt to explore the following relationships among major variables investigated in this study:

a. Management practices and management effectiveness
b. Degree of decentralization and management effectiveness
c. Manpower management practices (personnel practices) and management effectiveness.

Construct of Indices

To establish statistical relationships among these major variables, we constructed three different indices: (a) management practices; (b) decentralization; (c) manpower management practices; and (d) management effectiveness.

The factors evaluated for each index and the ranking of these factors are outlined in Tables 8-3, 8-5, 8-7 and 8-8.,

Briefly, we devised a three-point ranking scale for each of the factors evaluated in the four indices. A ranking of one point represents the most progressive practices or highest degree of effectiveness, while the ranking of three points represents the least progressive management practices or lowest effectiveness. The composite index for each company is computed by adding up the total points and dividing these by the total number of factors evaluated for each of the above indices. This gives us an index for each company ranging from a minimum of 1.0 (highly progressive practices or highest effectiveness) to a maximum of 3.0 (least progressive management practices or lowest effectiveness).

To explore statistical relationships among the above variables, Spearman's rank correlation coefficients were computed. These results are given in Tables 8-2, 8-4, and 8-6.

In summarizing, we find the following relationships among these variables:

Variables	*Spearman's Rank Correlation Coefficient*
1. Management Practices and Management Effectiveness	r = .82
2. Decentralization and Management Effectiveness	r = .66
3. Manpower Management Practices and Management Effectiveness	r = .80

TABLE 8-2. *Management Practices and Management Effectiveness (Spearman Rank Correlation)*

	Company Code #	Management Practices Index	Management Effectiveness Index	
U.S. Subsidiaries 01 to 09	01	1.58	1.90	
	02	1.00	1.00	
	03	1.00	1.00	
	04	1.71	1.50	
	05	2.42	2.90	
	06	1.00	1.10	
	07	1.92	1.20	
	08	1.00	1.00	
	09	1.42	1.70	
Local Companies 21 to 31	21	2.75	2.30	
	22	2.25	2.00	
	23	2.08	2.30	
	24	1.92	2.10	
	25	1.67	1.20	
	26	2.04	2.10	
	27	2.83	2.50	
	28	N.A.	N.A.	
	29	2.54	2.10	
	30	1.08	1.00	
	31	2.75	2.50	
Japanese Subsidiaries 41 to 47	41	1.71	2.00	
	42	2.38	2.10	
	43	2.25	2.80	
	44	2.04	2.20	
	45	2.25	1.50	
	46	1.67	1.30	
	47	2.29	1.70	r = .82

TABLE 8-3. *Ranking Scale of the Factors Evaluated for the Management Practices Index*

Factors Evaluated	Ranking Scale
1. Planning Orientation	
a. Long-range planning (5 years or more)	1
b. Medium and short-range (1 year)	2
c. Ad hoc basis	3

TABLE 8-3 (*continued*)

Factors Evaluated	Ranking Scale
2. *Quality Control*	
a. Formally and systematically done by qualified personnel	1
b. Formally done by unqualified personnel	2
c. Ad hoc basis – no quality control	3
3. *Equipment Maintenance*	
a. Systematically done by skilled personnel	1
b. Done by unskilled and semiskilled personnel	2
c. Done on an ad hoc basis	3
4. *Standard Settings in Production*	
a. Formally and systematically done	1
b. Partially done	2
c. Not done – ad hoc basis	3
5. *Standard Settings for White Collar Employees*	
a. Formally and systematically done	1
b. Partially done	2
c. Not done – ad hoc basis	3
6. *Standard Settings for Middle Management Personnel*	
a. Formally and systematically done	1
b. Partially done	2
c. Not done – ad hoc basis	3
7. *Cost Control*	
a. Qualified personnel – done for all or major products	1
b. Unqualified personnel – done for major products	2
c. Not done – ad hoc basis	3
8. *Budgeting and Resources Allocating*	
a. For entire firm – qualified personnel	1
b. Partially done for some departments – somewhat qualified personnel	2
c. Not done – ad hoc basis	3
9. *Leaders' Perceptions of Subordinates*	
a. Subordinates confident and trustworthy	1
b. Subordinates somewhat confident and trustworthy	2
c. Subordinates not confident and trustworthy	3

TABLE 8-4. *Decentralization and Management Effectiveness*

	Company Code #	Decentralization Index	Management Effectiveness Index
U.S. Subsidiaries 01 to 07	01	2.24	1.90
	02	1.94	1.00
	03	1.67	1.00
	04	2.91	1.50
	05	2.79	2.90
	06	1.61	1.10
	07	1.97	1.20
	08	1.97	1.00
	09	1.88	1.70
Local Companies 21 to 31	21	2.79	2.30
	22	2.30	2.00
	23	2.33	2.30
	24	2.33	2.10
	25	2.03	1.20
	26	2.00	2.10
	27	2.70	2.50
	28	N.A.	N.A.
	29	2.70	2.10
	30	1.85	1.00
	31	2.94	2.50
Japanese Subsidiaries 41 to 47	41	2.94	2.00
	42	2.52	2.10
	43	2.39	2.80
	44	2.12	2.20
	45	2.48	1.50
	46	2.64	1.30
	47	1.88	1.70 r = .66

TABLE 8-5. *Ranking Scale of the Factors Evaluated for the Decentralization Index*

Factors	Points
1. Layers of hierarchy (top executive to blue-collar worker)	
a. 3 to 6 layers	1
b. 7 to 10 layers	2
c. 11 and more layers	3

TABLE 8-5 (*continued*)

Factors	Points
2. *Locus of decision-making (major policies)*	
a. Broad representation of executives and stockholders	1
b. Top level executive committees	2
c. Chief executive or owner only	3
3. *Locus of decision-making (sales policies)*	
a. Executive committee with representation of all functional areas	1
b. Chief executive with the help of sales manager	2
c. Top executive/owner only	3
4. *Locus of decision-making (product-mix)*	
a. Executive committee with representation of all functional areas	1
b. Chief executive with the help of production/marketing manager	2
c. Chief executive/owner only	3
5. *Locus of decision-making (standard setting in production)*	
a. Executive committee with representation of all functional areas	1
b. Chief executive with production manager	2
Production manager only	
c. Chief executive only	3
6. *Locus of decision-making (manpower policies)*	
a. Executive committee with representation of all functional areas	1
b. Chief executive with personnel manager	2
c. Chief executive only	3
7. *Locus of decision-making (selection of executive personnel)*	
a. Executive committee with representation of all functional areas	1
b. Chief executive with personnel manager	2
c. Chief executive only	3
8. *The degree of participation in long-range planning*	
a. All levels of executives-top, middle, and lower	1
b. Top level with some representation of middle level executives	2
c. Chief executive/owner only	3
9. *The degree of information-sharing*	
a. Considerable-general memos on all major aspects of the company's operation	1
b. Fair-special reports on the company's affairs distributed to only top level and middle level executives	2
c. Little-all information kept secret from everybody except few top level executives	3

TABLE 8-6. *Manpower Management Practices and Management Effectiveness*

	Company Code #	Manpower Management Index	Management Effectiveness Index	
U.S.	01	2.22	1.90	
Subsidiaries	02	1.56	1.00	
01 to 09	03	1.11	1.00	
	04	1.56	1.50	
	05	2.67	2.90	
	06	1.33	1.10	
	07	1.67	1.20	
	08	1.11	1.00	
	09	1.67	1.70	
Local	21	2.67	2.30	
Companies	22	2.33	2.00	
21 to 31	23	2.22	2.30	
	24	2.11	2.10	
	25	1.67	1.20	
	26	2.57	2.10	
	27	2.87	2.50	
	28	N.A.	N.A.	
	29	2.44	2.10	
	30	1.33	1.00	
	31	3.00	2.50	
Japanese	41	2.11	2.00	
Subsidiaries	42	2.00	2.10	
41 to 47	43	1.89	2.80	
	44	1.78	2.20	
	45	1.89	1.50	
	46	2.11	1.30	
	47	2.22	1.70	r = .80

TABLE 8-7. *Ranking Scales for the Factors Evaluated for Manpower Management Index*

Factors	Points
1. Manpower planning	
a. Formalized and rationalized	1
b. Somewhat formalized and rationalized	2
c. Ad hoc basis	3
2. Employee selection	
a. Formalized and rationalized	1
b. Somewhat formalized and rationalized	2
c. Ad hoc basis	3
3. Compensation and employee benefits	
a. Formalized and rationalized	1
b. Somewhat formalized and rationalized	2
c. Ad hoc basis	3
4. Employee appraisal	
a. Formalized and rationalized	1
b. Somewhat formalized and rationalized	2
c. Ad hoc basis	3
5. Employee training and development for management and supervisory personnel	
a. Formalized and rationalized	1
b. Somewhat formalized and rationalized	2
c. Ad hoc basis	3
6. Training and development for blue collar workers	
a. Formalized and rationalized	1
b. Somewhat formalized and rationalized	2
c. Ad hoc basis	3

TABLE 8-8. *Ranking Scales for the Factors Evaluated for the Management Effectiveness Index*

Factors	Points
1. Management ability to attract and retain high-level manpower	
a. Able to attract and retain highly trained personnel	1
b. Able to attract and retain moderately trained personnel	2
c. Not able to attract and retain even moderately trained personnel	3

TABLE 8-8 (*continued*)

Factors	Points
2. *Employee morale and satisfaction in work*	
a. Excellent morale and highly satisfied	1
b. Average morale and somewhat satisfied	2
c. Poor morale and highly dissatisfied	3
3. *Employee turnover and absenteeism*	
a. 0 to 5%	1
b. 6 to 11%	2
c. 12% and more	3
4. *Interpersonal relationships in organizational settings*	
a. Very cooperative	1
b. Somewhat cooperative	2
c. Hardly cooperative	3
5. *Departmental relationships (Subsystem relationship)*	
a. Very cooperative	1
b. Somewhat cooperative	2
c. Hardly cooperative	3
6. *The executive's perception of the firm's overall objectives*	
a. Total optimization (achievement of the firm's objectives is perceived as most important)	1
b. Suboptimization (achievement of the departmental objectives is preferred)	2
c. Achievement of the departmental objectives is the ultimate goal	3
7. *Utilization of high-level manpower*	
a. Policy-making and future planning	1
b. Coordination with other departments	2
c. Routine work, day-to-day work, and excessive supervision of subordinate's duties	3
8. *Organizational effectiveness in adapting to the external environments*	
a. Able to adapt without much difficulty	1
b. Able to adapt partially with some difficulty	2
c. Not able to adapt	3

The nature of the above relationships clearly suggests that the utilization of advanced management practices *does lead* to higher management effectiveness. Data gathered for this study and for other studies undertaken in developing countries [8] support this assertion. In other words, empirical evidence indicates that the firm which undertakes long-range planning, formulates major policies and utilizes these as guidelines and control mechanisms, administers other control devices (such as cost and budgetary control, quality control, etc.), delegates decision-making authority to subordinates, and utilizes a consultative type of leadership will achieve higher managerial effectiveness. We contend that many advanced management practices found in U.S. industries are not necessarily dysfunctional or useless when applied to enterprises in Taiwan, or for that matter, to enterprises in other developing nations. We are also inclined to believe, based on the results of this study, that advanced management practices and know-how are transferable to the industrial enterprises in Taiwan.

[8] *Ibid.*

APPENDIX A

INTERVIEW GUIDE

	Card 1 Column
1. General Information	
Company's Identification —	1–2
Company	
a. U.S. Subsidiary —	3
b. Taiwanese Co. —	
c. Japanese Co. —	
2. Type of Industry	
a. Chemical and Pharmaceutical —	4
b. Petroleum —	
c. Light Engineering Products —	
d. Heavy Engineering Products —	
e. Electrical - Consumer Non-Durable Goods —	
f. Electrical - Consumer Durable Goods —	
g. Rubber - Tires —	
h. Soaps and Cosmetics —	
i. Soft Drinks, Canned Products —	
j. Textiles —	
k. Others —	
—	
—	
3. Size	
a. Number of Employees —	5
b. Sales —	
c. Relative size	
Big —	
Medium —	
Small —	

Column

4. Persons Interviewed

____
____
____

Date

7. Who are Responsible for Documentation and Communication

a. Policy Committee —
b. Top Executives —
c. Divisional Manager — 15
d. Supervisor —
e. Nobody —
f. Not Certain/Unclear —

8. Frequency of Review

a. Yearly — 16
b. Twice a Year —
c. Quarterly —
d. Monthly —
e. Never —
f. Ad hoc —

MANAGEMENT PROCESS VARIABLES

PLANNING FOR THE FUTURE

9. Length of Planning

a. Five years or more — 17
b. 1-2 years —
c. Ad hoc —
d. No planning at all —
e. Total score —

10. Resulting Plans

a. Systematic detailed plans with aid of computers — 18
b. Systematic detailed plans without aid of computers —
c. Systematic but limited —
d. Limited forecasts randomly done —
e. No Planning at all —
f. Total score —

Column

11. *Nature of Planning*
  a. Financial — 19
  b. Product —
  c. Plant —
  d. Comb. 1 & 2 —
  e. Comb. 2, 3 —
  f. Comb. 1, 3 —
  g. All three —
  h. none, random —
  Totale score —

12. *Planning objectives:* Why do you plan?
  a. For Long-term Growth — 20
  b. For Profit and Service —
  c. To Seek Direction —
  d. To Offer Employment —
  e. Total Score —

13. *Participation in Planning Process*
  a. Top Level Executives only — 21
  b. Top Level and Middle Level Executives —
  c. Top, Middle and Lower Level Executive —
  d. Total score —

14. *Information-Sharing in Planning Process*
  a. Confidential memos/verbal — 22
  b. Special reports, circulated restrictively —
  c. General/special reports circulated widely —
  d. Total score —

15. *Frequency of Review of Plans*
  a. Monthly — 23
  b. Quarterly —
  c. Semi-annually —
  d. Annually —
  e. Ad hoc —
  f. No Information —
  g. Total Score —

16. *What data is generated for long-range planning?*
  a. Detailed forecasts for all products — 24
  b. Some departmental forcasts only —

Column

c. Causal ideas/forecasts —
d. Not much —
Total Score —

17. Socio-economic, political, legal and cultural factors affecting planning process

a. Economic Stability — 25
b. Price Spiral —
c. Uncertainties about the availability of raw material —
d. Govt. control on prices and raw material —
e. Political Situation —
f. Market Conditions —
g. Lack of Knowledge on part of Executives —
h. Other factors —

ORGANIZATION

ORGANIZATION STRUCTURE

18. Layers of Hierarchy

a. 15 and more — 26
b. 8 to 15 —
c. 5 to 7 —

19. Authority Definition

a. Via charts and manuals — 27
b. Only verbally —
c. Not clear-cut —

20. When do you change organization structure? (Forces which brought changes)

a. Discovery of org. inefficiency — 28
b. Economic/social —
c. Personality whims —
d. Random – Unknown —
e. Other —

Column

GENERAL INFORMATION

ORGANIZATION STRUCTURE ASPECT

21 *Obtain the size of the enterprise and its sub-units.*

22. (*To infer delegation of authority*)
  a. What does manager do? (observe activities)
  b. What does assistant manager do? (observe activities)
  c. What does production manager do? (observe activities)
  d. What do supervisors and foremen do? (observe activities)

23. a. *Do you have an organization chart?* (*Obtain it and any other manuals available*)
  — Yes — No 29
  b. How are activities grouped in this organization?
  — function — geography — other (specify) 30
  c. Are there any "Service Departments"?
  — Yes — No
  d. To whom do they report? 31
  — General management — Department Heads
  — others 32

24. a. *Are there any staff positions, as opposed to line positions, in the organization structure?*
  — Yes — No 33
  b. How many are there and to whom do they report?
  c. What is their authority?
  — Recommending — Gather Data — Set Policy 34
  d. Do any supervisors in one department, line or staff, have any direct or indirect authority in other departments? (Looking for functional authority here)
  — Yes — No 35

25. *To whom do you report?* (*Further varification from the executive/personnel interviewed about overlapping of authority*)
  a. Does any other supervisor overlap your authority?
  — Much — Some — None 36
  b. How do you know whart your authority is?
  — Verbal — Written — Learned on job 37

26. a. *What use is made of committees in your organization?*
  — Many — Some — None 38

		Column
	b. What authority do they have? — Recommend — Plan — Execute — Cordinate	39
	c. What use is made of conferences in the company (or in your department)?	40
27.	a. *Have you been able to utilize informal groups to the benefit of the organization?* — Yes — No — None If *Yes*, how? ——	41
	b. Have they caused any problems for the company? — Yes — No	
28.	a. *Have there been any changes to the organization structure in the past 5 years? What?* — Many — Some — None	42
	b. What caused these changes? — Market & Eco. Forces — Exec. Personality	43
	c. Are you contemplating or considering any change? Why? — Yes — No	
	d. Who approves the establishment of new departments or new divisions?	44
29.	*How are the Budgeting and Cost Accounting Departments organized?*	45
30.	*How is the Personnel Department organized?*	46
31.	*How are the Purchasing and Sales Departments organized?*	47
32.	*How is the Production Department organized?*	48

FURTHER INFORMATION TO INFER THE DEGREE OF CENTRALIZATION-DECENTRALIZATION/DELEGATION OF AUTHORITY

			Column
33.	*Major Policy-Making: Who Makes Them?*		
	a. Owner/Top Executives	—	49
	b. Executive Committee (with Top Level Executives only)	—	
	c. Generals Committee, made of all levels of personnel	—	
	d. Top and Middle level Executives	—	
	e. Nobody; specific policies are made on ad hoc basis	—	
	f. Total score	—	
34.	*Who makes policies regarding marketing?*		
	a. Owner/Top Executives only	—	50
	b. Committee made of Functional Managers	—	

Column

c. Functional managers concerned —
d. Committee made of marketing dept. personnel —
e. Not clear cut —
f. Different for different departments —
g. Others —
Total score —

35. Policy-making for Product-line

a. Top Level Executive only — 51
b. Executive Committee of Functional Managers —
c. General Executive Committee —
d. Functional Manager —
e. Functional Manager's Committee —
f. Ad hoc, not clear-cut —
Total score —

36. Selection and Promotion of Executive Personnel

a. Top Executive/owner —
b. Top Executive Committee 52
c. General Committee —
d. Functional manager concern —
e. Ad hoc, not clear-cut —
Total score —

37. Selection and Promotion of Clerical Workers

a. Top Executive/owner — 53
b. Top Executive Committee —
c. General committee —
d. Functional manager —
e. Supervisor —
f. Departmental committee —
g. Ad hoc —
Total score —

38. Selection and Promotion of Blue-collar Employees

a. Top Executive/owner —
b. Top Executive Committee —
c. General Committee —
d. Functional Manager —
e. Supervisor —
f. Departmental committee —
g. Ad hoc —
h. Total score —

39. Who Sets Standards?

	1. For Production of Goods/ Services Column 55	2. For Executive Personnel Column 56	3. For Blue-Collar Workers Column 57	4. For Office Employees (clerical workers) Column 58
a. Top Executive/owner	—	—	—	—
b. Top Executive Committee	—	—	—	—
c. General Committee	—	—	—	—
d. Supervisor	—	—	—	—
e. Departemental Committee	—	—	—	—
f. Ad hoc	—	—	—	—
g. Others	—	—	—	—
Total score	—	—	—	—

40. Further Measures of Decentralization (Adapted from Schwitter-Pheysey's Project)

AUTHORITY (CENTRALIZATION: AUTONOMY OF THE ORGANIZATION)

WHO HAS AUTHORITY TO DECIDE:

(Authority = action can be taken on the decision without waiting for confirmation from above, even if the decision is later ratified at a higher level.)

At what level of the organization does the authority rest to decide:

	AUTHORITY TO DECIDE	LEVEL OF AUTHORITY
a.*	THE TOTAL AMOUNT OF WHITE COLLAR AND MANAGERIAL PERSONNEL THAT OUGHT TO BE EMPLOYED	
b.	APPOINTMENT OF SUPERVISORY STAFF FROM OUTSIDE THE ORGANIZATION (EX-ternal recruitment)	
c.	PROMOTION OF SUPERVISORY STAFF	
d.	SALARIES OF SUPERVISORY STAFF	
e.	TO DISMISS A SUPERVISOR	

AUTHORITY (CENTRALIZATION: AUTONOMY OF THE ORGANIZATION)

	AUTHORITY TO DECIDE	LEVEL OF AUTHORITY
f.	TO DETERMINE A NEW PRODUCT OR SERVICE	
g.	TO DETERMINE MARKETING TERRITORIES COVERED (where new or existing outputs are to be marketed)	
h.	THE EXTENT OF MARKET SHARE AND TYPE OF MARKET TO BE AIMED FOR	
i.	THE PRICE OF THE OUTPUT	
j.	WHAT TYPE, OR WHAT BRAND NEW EQUIPMENT IS TO BE USED	
k.*	WHAT TYPES OF EXPENDITURES SHOULD BE RECORDED UNDER VARIOUS COST HEADINGS	
l.	WHAT SHALL BE INSPECTED (i.e. to what the inspection system, if any, shall be applied)	
m.	WHAT OPERATIONS SHALL BE WORK STUDIED	
n.	WHICH SUPPLIERS OF MATERIALS ARE TO BE USED	
o.	BUYING PROCEDURES (what procedure is to be followed when buying materials, etc.)	
p.	TRAINING METHODS TO BE USED (how training shall be done)	
q.	WHAT AND HOW MANY WELFARE FACILITIES ARE TO BE PROVIDED	
r.	TO SPEND UNBUDGETED OR UNALLOCATED MONEY ON CAPITAL ITEMS (using money not previously ear-marked for a particular purpose for what would be classed as current expenditure)	
s.	TO SPEND UNBUDGETED OR UNALLOCATED MONEY ON REVENUE ITEMS (using money not previously earmarked, for what would be classed as current expenditure	

AUTHORITY (CENTRALIZATION: AUTONOMY OF THE ORGANIZATION)

	AUTHORITY TO DECIDE	LEVEL OF AUTHORITY
t.	TO ALTER RESPONSIBILITIES/AREAS OF WORK OF SPECIALIST DEPARTMENTS	
u.	TO ALTER RESPONSIBILITIES/AREAS OF WORK OF LINE DEPARTMENTS	
v.	TO CREATE A NEW DEPARTMENT (functional specialist or line)	
w.	TO CREATE A NEW JOB (functional specialist or line, of any status, probably signified by a new job title)	

Column
59

SOME OFFSET QUESTIONS ON DECENTRALIZATION

What do the following concepts/words mean to you?
Participative management —— 60
"Y" theory of management ——
Project management ——
"X" theory of management ——

MANAGEMENT PROCESS VARIABLES

Controlling

Setting of Standards. See Question 39, (1), (2), (3), (4)

41. *Who usually Discovers Deviations from the Established Standards? (X-Y Theory in Action)*
    a. Top Executive/Owner — 61
    b. Executive Committee —
    c. Functional manager —
    d. Departmental head —
    e. Foreman —
    f. Supervisor —
    g. Individual himself —

42. *What types of feedback systems are being used?*
    1. Medium of Feedback System
        a. by written memos — 62
        b. verbal report —

Column

c. casual hints —
d. private consultation —
e. other means (specify) —
——

2. The origin of Feedback Systems; (where does it originate?)
   a. Top Executive/Owner — 63
   b. Executive committee —
   c. Staff department e.g. accountant, controller, quality control, etc. —
   d. Departmental manager —
   e. Foreman/Supervisor —
   f. Individual worker himself decides the deviation and corrects himself —
   g. Others (specify) —

CONTROL TECHNIQUES USED

43. Cost Control Technique

a. Cost Accounting
   1. In what areas is cost accounting accomplished?
      — done for all products — done for major products 64
      — done at random — not done
   2. Who does cost accounting?
      — qualified personnel, separate department 65
      — qualified personnel, in respective departments
      — unqualified personnel in respective departments
      — unqualified personnel in separate departments
      — manager or department head himself
      — none

b. Budgeting and Resource Allocation
   1. For what purposes is this done? 66
      — for entire firm — for each plant
      — for each department — for each product
      — none
   2. Who does it?
      — Department with qualified people or controller 67
      — Top management and/or committee
      — Manager himself — Department
      — Others Specified — None

c. Job and/or Time Study Standards
   1. Production – Who does it?

	Column
— Separate time and motion study department	68
— Foreman (supervisor) — None	
— Others (specify)	
2. White Collar Workers - Who does it?	69
— Separate time and motion study department	
— Foreman (supervisor) — None	
— Others (specify)	
d. Equipment Maintenance - Who does it?	
— Separate Dept (skilled personnel)	70
— Separate Dept. (unskilled personnel)	
— Department Concern	
— Ad hoc	
44. *Research and Development*	
a. Do you spend a fixed percentage of your sales on research and development?	71
— Yes — No If Yes, how much?	
— 0–1%	
— 1–2%	
— 2–3%	
— More than 3%	
b. If not, how do you determine the overall level of research and development expenditures?	72
— What we can afford	
— Percentage of Profits	
— Meet Competitors	
c. How do you determine which research projects will be funded within your research and development budget?	
— Research department judgment	73
— Top managers' judgment	
— As per requirement of consumer	
— As per requirement of governmental authorities	
d. How many new products/processes have you developed in the last five years?	
— 25 and more	74
— 10–24	
— 1–9	
— none	
e. What is the percentage of total sales attributed to these new products?	
— 75–100%	75
— 50–74	
— 25–49	
— 10–24	
— 0–9	
— Insignificant	

Column

f. What other innovations has the company been undertaking/undertaken in the last five years? 76

____

____

____

____

g. What degree of automation and/or modernation has taken place in the company's operations?
1. Complete overhaul of machinery — 77
2. Considerable overhaul of machinery —
3. Some overhaul of machinery —
4. Complete overhaul of data processing (introduction of computer for accounting, budget, controlling, etc.) —
5. Some changes in data processing —
6. Considerable changes in organizational arrangements (what changes; specify) —
7. Some changes in organizational arrangements (what changes; specify) —
8. Ad hoc changes, uncoordinated —
9. No changes at all —

h. Who decides innovation, automation, and modernation?
1. Top executive/owner — 78
2. Executive committee —
3. General committee —
4. Ad hoc —
5. Others (specify) —

Column

LEADERSHIP

Card 2: Company's Identification:

45. Types of prevailing leadership 1–2

	Top Level Column 6	Middle Level Column 7	Supervisory Level Column 8
a. Considerably democratic	—	—	—
b. Somewhat democratic	—	—	—
c. Considerably autocratic	—	—	—
d. Somewhat autocratic	—	—	—
e. Considerably bureaucratic	—	—	—
f. Somewhat bureaucratic	—	—	—
g. Confused, not clear-cut; depends upon person	—	—	—

Comments (Record the impression or executives' comments about leadership role) 9

46. Manager's (leader's) perception of subordinates

A. At Top Level
- a. Leader perceives subordinates as confident and trustworthy — 10
- b. Leader perceives subordinates as somewhat confident and trustworthy —
- c. Leader perceives subordinates as not confident and trustworthy —

B. At Middle Level
- a. Leader perceives subordinates as confident and trustworthy — 11
- b. Leader perceives subordinates as somewhat confident and trustworthy —
- c. Leader perceives subordinates as not confident and trustworthy —

C. At Lower Level (supervisory level)
- a. Leader perceives subordinates as confident and trustworthy — 12

Column

b. Leader perceives subordinates as somewhat confident and trustworthy —
c. Leader perceives subordinates as not confident and trustworthy —

MANAGEMENT PROCESS VARIABLES

MANPOWER MANAGEMENT
(Staffing Policies and Practices)

MANPOWER MANAGEMENT POLICIES

47. *Are there specific policies about manpower management? (personnel policies)*
— Yes — No 13
If yes, who formulates them?
a. Top executive/owner — 14
b. Top executive committee —
c. General committee —
d. Personnel manager —
e. Ad hoc, undiscernable —
f. Other (specify) —

48. *Main objectives of personnel policies*
a. To satisfy the objectives of individual participants as well as organizational objectives — 15
b. To select right individuals —
c. To avoid trouble-makers —
d. No specific objectives —

SELECTION PROCEDURES

49. *What are the methods that you use to recruit your executive personnel?*
a. Intensive interviews with the help of outside consultants — 16
b. Intensive interviews by the executive committee —
c. Intensive interviews by the personnel manager/staff or functional managers —
d. Simple interviews/questionnaire —
e. Ad hoc, depending on the manager's concern —

50. *Who selects supervisory personnel?*
a. Top executive/owner — 17
b. Executive committee —
c. Personnel manager —

		Column
d. Functional manager/foreman	—	
e. Personnel manager/functional manager	—	
f. Ad hoc; not clear cut	—	

51. Who selects clerical workers?

a. Top executive/owner	—	18
b. Executive committee	—	
c. General staffing committee	—	
d. Personnel manager	—	
e. Functional manager concern	—	
f. Personnel manager/functional manager	—	
g. Supervisor/head clerk	—	
h. Others (specify)	—	

52. Who selects blue-collar workers?

a. Top executive/owner	—	19
b. Executive committee	—	
c. General staffing committee	—	
d. Personnel manager	—	
e. Functional manager concern	—	
f. Personnel manager/functional manager	—	
g. Supervisor/head clerk	—	
h. Others (specify)	—	

53. How do the methods used in recruiting executives differ from those used to recruit lower levels of personnel?
(comments) 20

54. What criteria do you use in selecting individuals who have been recruited for management positions?
— Education — Training and Experience 21
— Age — Market contacts — Family ties
— Other

55. What are the criteria that you use for promoting personnel?

Education and training	—	22
Years of experience	—	
Both	—	
Ability to get along with others	—	
Technical ability	—	
Not clear-cut	—	

56. What techniques are used in your personnel appraisal system?

No formal appraisal system	—	23
Standard forms	—	
Periodic reports from supervisor	—	
Executive committee	—	
Others (specify)	—	

		Column
57. *How do you provide for managerial succession?*		
No formal method	—	24
Management succession chart	—	
Job rotation	—	
Other	—	
58. *Who makes executive promotion decisions?*		
President	—	25
President and executive committee	—	
President with personnel manager	—	
President with personnel manager and functional manager	—	
Special promotion committee	—	
Ad hoc	—	
A. If by a committee, who are the members of the committee?		26
B. Who makes promotion decisions at lower management levels?		
President	—	27
Department head or functional manager	—	
Department head with personnel manager	—	
Department head with staffing committee	—	
Ad hoc	—	
Others (specify)	—	
C. Who makes promotion decisions for blue-collar workers?		
Department head or functional manager	—	28
Department head with personnel manager	—	
Staffing committee	—	
Supervisor	—	
Ad hoc; not clear cut	—	
D. Who makes hire and fire decisions for top level executives?		
President	—	29
Executive committee	—	
Personnel manager	—	
Special promotion committee	—	
Others	—	
E. Who makes hire and fire decisions for middle management?		
President	—	30
Department head or functional manager	—	
Department head with personnel manager	—	
Department head with staffing committee	—	
Others (specify)	—	
F. Who makes hire and fire decisions for clerical workers?		
Department head or functional manager	—	31
Department head with personnel manager	—	

		Column
Staffing committee	—	
Supervisor	—	
Others (specify)	—	

G. Who makes hire and fire decisions for blue-collar workers?

Department manager or functional manager	—	32
Department manager with personnel manager	—	
Other	—	

59. *What criteria are used in your personnel appraisal system for management positions?*

Education	—	33
Extensive Experience (10 years plus)	—	
Ability to get along with others	—	
Aggressiveness	—	
Company loyalty	—	
Other (specify)	—	

60. *Do you use either written or verbal job descriptions in your selection process?*

Written	—	34
Written classification with no specific positions	—	
Verbal	—	

61. *Who writes job descriptions?*

Personnel department	—	35
Motion and time study engineers	—	
Supervisors	—	
Nobody	—	
Other	—	

62. *How do you determine the levels of compensation for various jobs within your firm?*

Job description	—	36
Recommendation of the supervisor	—	
Pay goes with position	—	
Going wage	—	
Market forces	—	
Other	—	

63. *Do you have any type of formal training programs?*

— Yes — No 37

For what level?

Operator	—
Supervisors	—
Jr. Management	—
Sr. Management	—

64. *Which employees participate in which types of training programs.*

	Column: 38 Operators	Column: 39 Supervisor	Column: 40 Jr. Managers	Column: 41 Sr. Managers
On-the-job				
Formal – in Company				
Formal – Outside				
On-the-job plus in company				
On-the-job plus outside				
Job rotation				
Training for promotion purposes				

	Column
65. *Who runs the training program?*	42
How many people are employed in running the training program at each stage above?	43
66. *What percentage of the total average company man-hours per week are utilized for training purposes?*	
16–20% —	44
11–15% —	
5–10% —	
1– 5% —	
67. *Do you have a layoff status for your employees?*	
Yes — No —	45
68. *Under what conditions are employees dismissed?*	
Absence —	
Incompetence —	
Stealing —	
Insubordination —	
Market forces —	
Other —	
69. *How long does it take to dismiss employees who are no longer needed?*	46

	Column
70. *What is the procedure for dismissal?*	47
71. *Have you experienced difficulty in recruiting and keeping personnel with specific skills or abilities?*	48
— Yes — No	
A. Which skills? ________________________________	
________________________________	
B. For what reason?	
Non-availability of skilled personnel —	49
Lack of training and educational facilities in the community —	
Low wage scales —	
Low level of fringe benefits —	
Some unfavorable management policy (specify) —	
Other —	
72. *Which skills and abilities have been the most difficult to find and keep?*	
Technical personnel —	50
Managerial personnel with special skills —	
Managerial personnel in general —	
Blue collar, skilled —	
Unskilled —	
73. *Please give some estimate of your turnover rate for the last 5 years.*	
Blue collar —	51
Clerical —	
Supervisors —	
Jr. Management —	
Middle Management —	
Top Management —	
74. *What is your estimate of the rate of absenteeism at the various levels within your firm?*	
Operator —	
Supervisory —	52
Jr. Management —	
Sr. Management —	
75. *What is your personnel turnover rate among supervisors?*	53
76. *What are the socio-economic, legal and cultural factors which, in your opinion, affect employee morale and satisfaction in work?*	54

Column

77. Factors affecting the selection and promotion procedures concerning your high-level manpower? 55

78. What types of financial compensation do you use?

	For Workers	For Clerical Employees	For Executive group	56–58
Salaries	—	—	—	
Hourly wages	—	—	—	
Bonuses	—	—	—	
Stock options	—	—	—	
Other	—	—	—	

79. How do you deal with your employees?
Through union representation — 59
Through first line supervisors —
Both —

80. If you do not have a union at your firm, has there been any recent attempt by union organizers to enter your firm?
— Yes — No 60
A. What are these unions?
B. How did you handle their attempts at organizing unions? 61

MANAGEMENT EFFECTIVENESS
(Behavioral variables)

80. A. *Employee Morale and Satisfaction in Work*
(To infer, interview at least 50 workers in each company)
a. Excellent morale and employees highly satisfied — 62
b. Average morale and employees somewhat satisfied —
c. Poor morale and employees highly dissatisfied —
B. Employee Productivity: Obtain any measure of productivity available, e.g. 63
a. Number of items produced per worker 64
b. Cost per unit
c. Scrap loss or waste material
d. Improvements made by the workers themselves
e. Others (specify)
C. Socio-economic, political, legal, and cultural variables affecting employee morale and satisfaction in work and productivity See 54
Management viewpoint 65
Other Expert's (e.g., Professor, business man, govt.

Column

leader) Viewpoint 66

Workers' Viewpoint 67

81. *Interpersonal Relationship: Attitudes of workers among themselves and among workers and supervisors (To infer, interview at least 50 workers and supervisors in each company)*

A. Among workers and supervisors

a. Very cooperative attitude toward each other — 68

b. Somewhat cooperative attitude toward each other —

c. Hostile attitude toward each other —

B. Among workers themselves

a. Very cooperative — 69

b. Somewhat cooperative —

c. Hostile attitudes —

C. Socio-economic, political, legal and cultural variables affecting interpersonal relationships

Management viewpoint

70

Other experts' viewpoint

Workers' viewpoint

82. *Labor Absenteeism rate (as percentage of total labor force employed; average of one year)*

a. 25% and more — 71

b. 15–24% —

c. 5–14% —

d. 4% or less —

83. *Labor turnover rate (as percentage of total labor force employed; average of one year)*

a. 25% and more — 72

b. 15–24% —

c. 5–14% —

d. 4% or less —

84. *Socio-economic, political, legal and cultural factors affecting absenteeism*

A. Management viewpoint 73

B. Other experts' viewpoint

C. Workers' viewpoint

85. *Organizational effectiveness in hiring and retaining trained managerial and technical personnel (observe from executives interviewed as well ask them about it)*

a. Able to hire and retain highly trained personnel — 74

Column

b. Able to hire and retain average trained personnel —
c. Not able to hire and retain even average trained personnel —

86. *Environmental factors (socio-economic, political, legal and cultural) affecting organizational ability to hire and retain trained personnel* 75

87. *Interdepartmental relationships (observe the Executives' behavior pattern, especially their viewpoint about other departments)*
a. Very cooperative — 76
b. Somewhat cooperative —
c. Poor cooperation —

88. *Environmental Factors Affecting Interdepartmental Relationships* 77

89. *Executives' perception (viewpoint) of the achievement of the firm's objectives*
a. Total optimization (achievement of the firm's objectives) is perceived as most important — 78
b. Sub-optimization (achievement of the departmental objectives) is preferred —
c. Achievement of the departmental objectives as ultimate goal —

90. *Environmental factors affecting interdepartmental relationships*

91. *Utilization of high-level manpower (interview only top executive and functional managers)*

A. What executives do
1. Policy-making and future planning — 79
2. Coordination with other departments —
3. Routine work, day-to-day work —
4. Excessive supervision with subordinate's duties —

B. Executive's enthusiasm and drive in his work
1. Enormous drive and enthusiasm — 80
2. Moderate drive and enthusiasm —
3. Doing work as part of living —

Card 3: Company's Identification 1–2

92. *Environmental factors affecting the utilization of high-level manpower* 6

		Column
93. *Organizational effectiveness in adapting to environmental conditions*		
a. Able to adapt without much difficulty	—	7
b. Able to adapt partially with some difficulty	—	
c. Not able to adapt	—	
d. Not discernible	—	

ENTERPRISE EFFECTIVENESS

94. *Obtain the following information:*		
a. Net profits of firm for last 5 years	—	8
b. Gross profits of firm for last 5 years	—	9
Gross sales of industry for last 5 years	—	10
c. Rate of return on equity of firm for last 5 years (year by year)	—	11
Average rate of return on equity for industry for last 5 years	—	12
d. Per cent increase in profits in last 5 years (year by year)	—	13
Average per cent increase in profits for the industry in last 5 years	—	14
e. Market share of the company in the main product line	—	15
Per cent increase in market share for the last 5 years	—	16
f. Market price of company's stock	—	17
Per cent increase in price of stock in last 5 years	—	18
g. Per cent increase in sales in last 5 years	—	19
Average per cent increase in sales for industry for last 5 years	—	20
h. Scrap loss	—	21
i. Worker's productivity	—	22
j. Number of new products in last 5 years	—	23
k. Number of new innovations in last five years	—	24
95. *Environmental factors affecting delegation of authority (decentralization process)*		25
96. *Environmental factors affecting planning process*		See column 25 card 1
97. *Environmental factors affecting controlling aspects*		26
98. *Environmental factors affecting staffing (selecting, appraisal, promoting employees) function*		27

Column

99. Environmental factors affecting leadership function (including direction) 28

100. Environmental factors affecting adaptation of advanced management know-how in industrial companies in Taiwan 29

COMMENTS

APPENDIX B

QUESTIONNAIRE*

Set 1. The following questions pertain to your "top management" philosophy and policies.

Please check in which of the following areas your top management makes policies.

a. Marketing: Price — Advertising Budget — Product Line —
b. Personnel: Selection — Training — Salaries — Relations —
c. Production: Technology — Purchasing — Controls —
d. Finance: Borrowing — Plant Investment — Acquisitions —

Are the policies explicit? Yes, always — Sometimes —
Are these policies written down? Yes — No —
Who writes them? —— Who reviews them? ——
How are they communicated? ——

Suppose there is a need for some change in existing policies in regard to the above areas. Can other persons than top managers suggest —, make specific recommendations — initiate changes —?
Has this happened before? How often, in the past?
Frequently — Occasionally — Seldom — Never —

The following are some hypothetical situations. Please indicate whether it is the top management (TM) or others (0) who have the final say in each situation. You can write TM or 0.

a. To purchase new equipment costing $50 —; costing $500 —; costing $5,000 —; costing $50,000 —.
b. To give a salary raise to a supervisory or staff worker, to the extent of 1% —; 3% —; 5% —; 12% —.
c. To introduce the following types of changes:
   A new policy regarding labor relations —
   A new policy to change accounting procedures —
   A new policy in the marketing procedure —
   A new policy in production methods —

* This questionnaire was designed after Mason Haire, *et al* questionnaire (Mason Haire, *et al*, *Managerial Thinking: An International Study* (New York: John Wiley and Sons, Inc., 1966) pp. 185–192. This was adapted by Professor S. B. Prasad of Ohio University. I am most thankful to these authors.

Set 2. The following question pertains to salary ratios. Please do not furnish any dollar figures. Just indicate the approximate ratios of salaries (excluding fringes and other compensation).

a. If the production worker's salary is 1:

	POSSIBLY
his supervisor's average salary is	— (2, 3, 4, 5, 6)
a middle manager's average salary is	— (4, 5, 6, 7, 8, 9)
a top manager's average salary is	— (9, 10, 11, 12, 13)

Set 3. How many divisions are there in your organizations? —
How many of these are headed by separate managers? —
How many middle-level managers report to these division managers? (on the average) ——
How are these divisions organized? That is, is there a principle or philosophy underlying these divisions? For example, profit center concept? — Other? —

Set 4. Are middle-level or top managers recruited from outside the company? Never — Rarely — Occasionally — Often —
Does seniority of the management men outweigh their managerial ability as a basis for promotion and higher compensation?
Never — Rarely — Occasionally — Often —

Set 5. The following questions pertain to management of subsidiaries in Taiwan abroad. Again, please do not furnish any financial information. Please complete the blanks simply by checking.
(Here, DECISIVE means final authority rests with the U.S. Parent Co.).
(Here, NEGLIGIBLE means final decision by subsidiary is independent of the views of the Parent Co. MODERATE is between these two)

	DECISIVE	MODERATE	NEGLIGIBLE
Overall management policy	—	—	—
Overall management structure	—	—	—

Set 6. The following refer to management *techniques* in the stated areas. Please indicate the degree to which the *techniques* of the subsidiaries are identical with those of the Parent Company.

	Closely	*Moderately*	*Negligibly*
a. Product Development-innovation	—	—	—
b. Production Planning & Control	—	—	—
c. Motivation of Workers	—	—	—
d. Budgeting (and Control)	—	—	—
e. Market Research	—	—	—
f. Measuring Manpower Performance	—	—	—
g. Long Range Planning	—	—	—
h. Cost Controlling	—	—	—
i. Manpower Training	—	—	—
j. Advertising (& Selling)	—	—	—

PLEASE INDICATE TO WHAT EXTENT DO YOU AGREE WITH THE FOLLOWING:

	Strongly Agree	Agree	Un-decided	Disagree	Strongly Disagree
1. The Chinese Executives, generally speaking, are inclined to look to the past and the present. American Executives see the present and the future.	—	—	—	—	—
2. Chinese Executives communicate less to "middle managers" than American Executives and thereby save "executive time."	—	—	—	—	—
3. American Executives seem to feel that human relations in Taiwan have an authoritarian and paternalistic flavor.	—	—	—	—	—
4. Education in modern management (in schools or in Company) is absolutely necessary for Chinese middle-level as well as top executives.	—	—	—	—	—
5. Management (and the Management Process) is essentially an "art" and can only be learned on the job if the man is well-educated.	—	—	—	—	—
6. Decision-making authority should be tightly held at the top level so that the Company can "get on with the job."	—	—	—	—	—
7. The fundamental measure of accomplishment in a company should be profit and profit is best assured when production and sales are stabilized.	—	—	—	—	—
8. Top Executives should never be recruited from outside the company.	—	—	—	—	—

	Strongly Agree	Agree	Undecided	Disagree	Strongly Disagree
9. In case of promotion (and salary increase) seniority should be more heavily weighted than other factors.	—	—	—	—	—
10. While democratic style of Management sounds good on paper, in order to accomplish company goals year after year, top Executives have to be assertive and dominate the views and thinking of other lower level Executives.	—	—	—	—	—
11. The average human being prefers to be directed, wishes to avoid responsibility and has relatively little ambition.	—	—	—	—	—
12. Leadership skills can be acquired by most people regardless of their particular inborn traits and abilities.	—	—	—	—	—
13. The use of rewards (salary, promotion, etc.) and punishment (demotion, etc.) is *not* the best way to get subordinates to do their defined work.	—	—	—	—	—
14. In a work situation, if the subordinates cannot influence me, then I lose some influence on them.	—	—	—	—	—
15. A good leader should give detailed and complete instructions to his subordinates rather than giving them merely general directions and depending on their initiative to work out the details.	—	—	—	—	—
16. Group goal-setting offers advantage that cannot be obtained by individual goal-setting.	—	—	—	—	—

	Strongly Agree	Agree	Un-decided	Disagree	Strongly Disagree
17. A superior should give subordinates only that information which is necessary for them to do their immediate tasks.	—	—	—	—	—
18. The superior's authority over his subordinates in an organization (company) is primarily economic.	—	—	—	—	—

THANK YOU VERY MUCH FOR COMPLETING THIS QUESTIONNAIRE. IF YOU WOULD LIKE TO REVIEW AND APPROVE OF A RESEARCH REPORT BASED ON THIS INFORMATION PLEASE INDICATE BELOW:

Yes — No —

DO I HAVE YOUR PERMISSION TO LIST YOUR AND YOUR COMPANY NAME AS THOSE COMPANIES WHICH PARTICIPATED IN THIS RESEARCH PROJECT?

Yes — No —

We will look at the report and then consider ____________________

PLEASE BE SURE TO COMPLETE THIS PART

Title of the executive completing this form ____________________

His age: — Born in (what country?) ____________________

NAME INDEX

SUBJECT INDEX

MIX
Papier aus verantwortungsvollen Quellen
Paper from responsible sources
FSC® C105338
FSC
www.fsc.org

If you have any concerns about our products,
you can contact us on
ProductSafety@springernature.com

In case Publisher is established outside the EU,
the EU authorized representative is:
Springer Nature Customer Service Center GmbH
Europaplatz 3, 69115 Heidelberg, Germany

Printed by Libri Plureos GmbH
in Hamburg, Germany